LB 1032.C56 '86
LB 3011.K64 '96

WITHDRAWN
UTSA LIBRARIES

COLUMBUS AND HIS DISCOVERY

OF

AMERICA

AMS PRESS
NEW YORK

JOHNS HOPKINS UNIVERSITY STUDIES

IN

HISTORICAL AND POLITICAL SCIENCE

HERBERT B. ADAMS, Editor

History is past Politics and Politics present History—*Freeman*

TENTH SERIES

X-XI

COLUMBUS AND HIS DISCOVERY

OF

AMERICA

BY HERBERT B. ADAMS, PH. D., and HENRY WOOD, PH. D.
Professors in the Johns Hopkins University.

BALTIMORE
THE JOHNS HOPKINS PRESS
October and November, 1892

Reprinted from the edition of 1892, Baltimore
First AMS EDITION published 1971
Manufactured in the United States of America

International Standard Book Number: 0-404-00287-0

Library of Congress Number: 70-149681

AMS PRESS INC.
NEW YORK, N.Y. 10003

CONTENTS.

		PAGE.
I.	ORATION BY PROFESSOR HERBERT B. ADAMS	7
II.	ORATION BY PROFESSOR HENRY WOOD	40
III.	THE FIRST JEW IN AMERICA, BY PROFESSOR M. KAYSERLING,	45
IV.	COLUMBUS IN ORIENTAL LITERATURE, BY DR. CYRUS ADLER,	51

APPENDIX.

I.	BIBLIOGRAPHIES OF THE DISCOVERY OF AMERICA, BY CHARLES WEATHERS BUMP	55
II.	PUBLIC MEMORIALS OF COLUMBUS, BY CHARLES WEATHERS BUMP	69

COLUMBUS AND HIS DISCOVERY OF AMERICA.

I.[1]

"Was this his face, and these the finding eyes
    That plucked a new world from the rolling seas?
Who, serving Christ, whom most he sought to please,
    Willed his one thought until he saw arise
Man's other home and earthly paradise—
    His early vision, when with stalwart knees
He pushed the boat from his young olive-trees,
    And sailed to wrest the secret of the skies?

"He on the waters dared to set his feet,
    And through believing planted earth's last race.
What faith in man must in our new world beat,
    Thinking how once he saw before his face
The West and all the host of stars retreat
    Into the silent infinite of space!"[2]

Those faithful, finding eyes of Columbus! For now four hundred years they have looked outward upon the westward

---

[1] This address, by Professor Herbert B. Adams, was given at the Peabody Institute, Monday evening, October 10, 1892, to the officers and students of the Johns Hopkins University, and their friends, at the opening of the seventeenth academic year.

[2] This noble poem, "On a Portrait of Columbus," by Professor George E. Woodberry, of Columbia College, first appeared in *The Century Magazine*, May, 1892. The fine portrait which accompanied Mr. Woodberry's poem in that number was a copy of the "Columbus" now preserved in the Museum of the Ministry of Marine at Madrid. The picture was shown in enlarged form to the audience during the reading of the poem and the paragraph immediately following it.

course of empire in the new hemisphere which he first opened to discovery and conquest. Our modern eyes seek in vain to arrest that steadfast, far-away gaze, which seems to be looking into a future beyond our own. In the radiant light of the four hundredth anniversary of the discovery of America, millions of men and women will look upon this man's face with curious or admiring eyes; but when this generation, and many hundred years shall have passed away, those "finding eyes" will still be shining on through art, and poetry and history, like stars in the firmament.

There is a certain immortality in a great deed, like that of Columbus, which makes the doer, even though in many respects an ordinary man of his time, forever memorable. The discovery of America has been called the greatest event in secular history. This dictum may shock the ancients and startle the moderns; but let the mind of reflecting students range at will, through the centuries, back and forth in the galleries of human achievement, and determine if you can what single secular deed even approximates in grandeur and far-reaching historic significance to the finding of a new world on this earth, with which planet alone history is concerned. What are all the conquests of antiquity, or the decisive battles and great inventions of mankind, compared with America, time's noblest offspring? The passage of Christopher Columbus across the western sea, bearing the weight of Christendom and European civilization, opened the way for the greatest migrations in human history, for the steady march of enlightened nations towards civil and religious liberty. The discovery of America was the first crossing of Oceanus, that great and murmuring stream, which flowed around the old Mediterranean world. Amid the groaning and travailing of human creation, men burst the confines of that outward sea and began to people new continents. I tell you, sirs, the modern history of Europe, with its long exodus of hungry, landless peoples, with its epoch-making wars, its revolutions in church and state, were conditioned by that one secular event called the discovery of America.

Great deeds in history do not, however, stand alone. High mountains, grand and imposing though they may seem to the distant beholder, are after all simply conspicuous parts of our common earth. The loftiest peaks descend gradually to foothills, upland plateaus, lower plains, and finally to the level of the all-uniting sea. Nothing is isolated in nature or in human achievement. Great discoverers are like mountain-climbers, who by the aid of material vantage-ground and human experience, ascend height upon height until at last they stand like stout Balboa, when, silent upon a peak in Darien, with eagle eye he stared at the Pacific.

The discovery of America was foreordained from the beginning of the old classic world, when geographical science first began to move, "but slowly, slowly, creeping on from point to point," around the headlands of the Mediterranean Sea. Six hundred years B. C. the bold Phœnician sailors, under Egyptian auspices, circumnavigated Africa, sailing from East to West around what we now call the Cape of Good Hope, and returning in three years past the pillars of Hercules, through the straits of Gibraltar. Five hundred years before Christ, Hanno, the Carthaginian, anticipated the Portuguese discovery of the Canary Islands and the west coast of Africa.

Pythagoras and the Greek philosophers taught that the world is round. Plato, inspired by current traditions, based perhaps on physical facts, wrote in his dialogues of the continent of Atlantis, which had been submerged in the western sea. Aristotle believed that the inhabited earth, *oikoumené gé*, was only one of several continents. He had the correct theory of the globe. Indeed, all modern discovery was anticipated in the following scientific statement: "In common speech," says Aristotle, "we speak of our world (*oikoumené*) as divided into continents and islands. This is wrong. The *oikoumené*, as known to us, is really a single island, lying in the midst of the Atlantic. Probably there are other similar *oikoumenai*, some larger than ours, some smaller, separated from it by the sea."

In his treatise on the Heavens (ii, 14), Aristotle said "those persons who connect the region in the neighborhood of the Pillars of Hercules with that towards India, and who assert that in this way the sea is *one*, do not assert things very improbable." Here is a full-orbed scientific idea which finally conquered and possessed the round world.[1] Greek thought was prophetic. Greek history foreshadowed the history of Europe, which is simply a greater Hellas, as America is an imperial and transatlantic Magna Graecia. Nothing of Greece doth fade but suffers a sea-change into something rich and strange. All our modern discoveries, colonization, politics, art, education, civilization, Christendom, the Oikoumenê, the great globe itself, are simply Greek ideas enlarged by historic processes of development.

> "The word unto the prophet spoken
> Was writ on tables yet unbroken;
> The word by seers or sibyls told,
> In groves of oak, or fanes of gold,
> Still floats upon the morning wind,
> Still whispers to the willing mind.

---

[1] "Greek speculation survived, though it missed reduction into practice. Strabo, who was master of all the geographical fact and theory of his time, was not likely to neglect Aristotle's memorable conjecture of more *oikoumenai* than one. With almost prophetic insight, he even improved on it. Besides a Terra Australis, such as Aristotle had indicated, he clearly foreshadowed the discovery of a Terra Occidentalis, occupying the same latitudes as the old *oikoumenê* itself. 'Possibly,' he says, 'the same temperate zone may contain two or more *oikoumenai*. It is even likely that such are to be found in the parallel of Athens.' Were this the case, the physical objection to the practicability of a westward voyage to India would probably cease: for the new *oikoumenai* might serve as stepping-stones to the westward explorer. This remarkable anticipation goes far to justify the words of an enthusiastic modern geographer, who declares that the nations of Europe from remote antiquity were gifted with a divine intuition which revealed to them another great world beyond their horizon, and whispered that this world was their natural patrimony. Aristotle had guessed at the plurality of *oikoumenai*: Strabo suggested the existence of another *oikoumenê* occupying the same latitudes as the old world, that is, the existence of America." (*History of the New World Called America*, vol. I, pp. 36–37, by Edward John Payne.) Strabo, i, 31, quoting Krates, speaks of the western voyage of Menelaos from Gades to India (Dr. A. Gudeman, Philological Association, J. H. U.)

We have been taught that Hebrew prophecy was history and Hebrew history was prophecy. There is a remarkable verse from Seneca, who has won eternal fame from Clio for these few words, once prophetic now historic:

> Venient annis saecula seris,
> Quibus Oceanus vincula rerum
> Laxet, et ingens pateat tellus,
> Tethysque novos detegat orbes,
> Nec sit terris ultima Thule.
> —*Medea*, 378–382.

In the Columbian library at Valladolid there is a copy of Seneca's tragedies published at Venice in 1510. Upon the margin of the verse from the Medea which has been quoted, Ferdinand, the son of Columbus, wrote in Latin, "This prophecy was fulfilled by my father, Christopher Columbus, the admiral, in 1492."

Dante was the poet-prophet of the Middle Ages and the historian of ancient culture. In the twenty-sixth canto of the Inferno, the Italian poet, under the guidance of the Latin Virgil, meets Odysseus, the Grecian type of Columbus, the adventurous navigator, who had sailed every sea. To Dante Odysseus narrates how once he and his companions steered westward past the pillars of Hercules, out upon the ocean, seeking a new world.

> "'O brothers, who amid a hundred thousand
> Perils,' I said, 'have come unto the West,
> Be ye unwilling to deny the knowledge,
> Following the sun, of the unpeopled world.
> Consider ye the seed from which ye sprang;
> Ye were not made to live like unto brutes,
> But for pursuit of virtue and knowledge.'
> So eager did I render my companions
> With this brief exhortation for the voyage,
> That then I hardly could have held them back."

They rowed away from the morning and made wings of their oars for a mad flight into another hemisphere. They came at last to a high mountain and a new land, but there arose a whirlwind and it smote upon the ship. Three times the vessel whirled about and then sank beneath the sea with all on board. Thus Odysseus and his companions came into the under world.

One century after the time of Dante there lived in the republic of Florence another poet-prophet, a contemporary of Savonarola and of Columbus. In a poem called the Greater Morning, Morgante Maggiore, this poet Pulci, who died five years before the discovery of America, made this remarkable prophecy, translated by Prescott in his " Ferdinand and Isabella," Vol. II, 117:

> "his bark
> The daring mariner shall urge far o'er
> The Western wave, a smooth and level plain,
> Albeit the earth is fashioned like a wheel.
> Man was in ancient days of grosser mould,
> And Hercules might blush to learn how far
> Beyond the limits he had vainly set
> The dullest sea-boat soon shall wing her way.
> Men shall descry another hemisphere,
> Since to one common centre all things tend;
> So earth, by curious mystery divine,
> Well balanced hangs amid the starry spheres.
> At our Antipodes are cities, states
> And thronged empires ne'er divined of yore."
> —Pulci, *Morgante Maggiore*, Canto 25: 22.

Turning from the poet-prophets, let us briefly notice the relation of schoolmen, churchmen, and scientific men to Columbus. In the year 1267 a Franciscan friar at Oxford collected from classical, Arabian and Hebrew literature the chief arguments concerning the possibility of reaching Asia by sailing westward from Europe. This Franciscan was Roger Bacon, the scholastic forerunner of Lord Bacon and a pioneer of experimental methods in science and philosophy. In his Opus Majus the great schoolman of Oxford wrote the following extraordinary summary of the best scientific views of the world's geography: "Aristotle says that there is not much ocean between the western parts of Spain and the eastern parts of India. He thinks that more than a fourth part of the surface of the globe is habitable. Averrhoes confirms this. Seneca says that this sea might be crossed in a few days with a favorable wind. Pliny says that people have actually sailed from the Arabian Gulf to Cadiz. Now the Arabian Gulf is a whole year's voyage from the Indian sea, so that it is clear that the eastern extremity of Asia cannot be a long way from us. The sea between Spain and Asia at any rate cannot possibly cover three-fourths of the surface of the globe. Besides, it is written in the fourth Book of Esdras, that six parts of the earth are habitable, and the seventh is covered with water. . . . Therefore I say that though the *oikoumené* of Ptolemy be confined within one-fourth of the globe's surface, more of that surface is really habitable. Aristotle must have known more than other people, because by Alexander's favor he sent out two thousand men to enquire about these matters. So must Seneca; for the Emperor Nero sent out people to explore in the same way. From all this it follows that the habitable surface of the earth must be considerable, and that which is covered with water but small."

In the year 1410, nearly one hundred and fifty years after Roger Bacon penned this remarkable passage, a famous churchman, Cardinal D'Ailly, Bishop of Cambrai, wrote an encyclopædic work called the *Imago Mundi*, in which all this geographical information is carefully repeated from the learned Franciscan of Oxford. Cardinal D'Ailly was president of the ecclesiastical commission which condemned John Huss to the stake in the year 1415, but that book called the *Imago Mundi* kindled in Spain a beaconlight which shot across the western sea. The book was not published until the year 1490 but manuscript copies of it were widely known in the second half of the fifteenth century. Doubtless Columbus, who could read Latin, was an early student of the Cardinal's work. Indeed Columbus owned a printed copy of this famous book and it is still preserved in the Columbian library at Seville with his own marginal notes.

The influence upon Columbus of his reading upon the subject of physical geography is clearly indicated in the following extract from the narrative of his third voyage, sent to Ferdinand and Isabella from the Island of Hispaniola: "I have always read, that the world comprising the land and the water was spherical, and the recorded experiences of Ptolemy and all others, have proved this by the eclipses of the moon, and other observations made from east to west, as well as by the elevation of the pole from north to south. But as I have already described, I have now seen so much irregularity, that I have come to another conclusion respecting the earth, namely, that it is not round as they describe, but of the form of a pear, which is very round except where the stalk grows, at which part it is most prominent."[1]

In one of his letters Columbus thus summarizes his reading of classical and Arabian authorities through the medium of the *Imago Mundi* of Cardinal D'Ailly: "Pliny writes that the sea and land together form a sphere, but that the ocean forms the greatest mass, and lies uppermost, while the earth is below and supports the ocean, and that the two afford a mutual support to each other, as the kernel of a nut is confined by its shell. The Master of scholastic history, in commenting upon Genesis, says, that the waters are not very extensive; and that although when they were first created they covered the earth, they were yet vaporous like a cloud, and that afterwards they became condensed, and occupied but small space: and in this notion Nicolas de Lira agrees. Aristotle says that the world is small, and the water very limited in extent, and that it is easy to pass from Spain to the Indies; and this is confirmed by Averrhoes, and by the Cardinal Pedro de Aliaco, who, in supporting this opinion,

---

[1] *Select Letters of Christopher Columbus*, translated and edited by R. H. Major, p. 134. Edition of 1870.

shows that it agrees with that of Seneca, and says that Aristotle had been enabled to gain information respecting the world by means of Alexander the Great, and Seneca by means of the Emperor Nero, and Pliny through the Romans; all of them having expended large sums of money, and employed a vast number of people, in diligent inquiry concerning the secrets of the world, and in spreading abroad the knowledge thus obtained. The said cardinal allows to these writers greater authority than to Ptolemy, and other Greeks and Arabs; and in confirmation of their opinion concerning the small quantity of water on the surface of the globe, and the limited amount of land covered by that water, in comparison of what had been related on the authority of Ptolemy and his disciples, he finds a passage in the third book of Esdras, where that sacred writer says, that of seven parts of the world six are discovered, and the other is covered with water." [1]

All science, like all literature, simply combines existing elements into fresh forms. Columbus breathed upon the dry bones of ancient and mediaeval geography, and they sprang together into vital form. A towering genius for discovery, beckoning him westward, seemed to arise before the mind's eye of that simple Genoese sailor, as he read the pages of the *Imago Mundi*, in which the geographical wisdom of the ancients had drifted to the western shore of Europe. Mr. Winsor, in his critical work on "Christopher Columbus: how he received and imparted the spirit of discovery," says, p. 457: "Bacon it was who gave that tendency to thought which, seized by Cardinal Pierre D'Ailly, and incorporated by him in his *Imago Mundi* (1410), became the link between Bacon and Columbus."

In an address before the Royal Geographical Society, in June, 1892, Mr. Clements R. Markham, an English naval officer, and a leading authority upon Columbus, represents him as one of the most skilful navigators of his time. The

---

[1] *Select Letters of Christopher Columbus*, pp. 144–146.

republic of Genoa was the centre of nautical science, and Columbus early became versed in all the mathematical and astronomical knowledge necessary for a good pilot and captain. It is very doubtful whether Columbus was educated, as some have said, at the University of Pavia; but he was an intelligent student and a persistent reader of cosmographical science. In 1501 he wrote: "At a very early age I became a sailor, and a sailor I have been ever since. . . . For forty years have I followed this calling. Whithersoever men have sailed to this day, thither have I also sailed. I have held traffic and converse with the wise and prudent, churchmen and laymen, Latins and Greeks, Jews and Moors. . . . During this time have I seen and made it my study to see, all writings, cosmography, histories, chronicles, philosophy and other arts, so that the hand of the Lord plainly opened my understanding to see that it was possible to sail from hence to the Indies, and set on fire my will for the execution thereof."

Columbus went to Portugal in 1472, at the age of 25. He went as young men now go to Chicago and the west. Lisbon was a city of enterprise and bold endeavor. For more than a hundred years skilful Genoese pilots, the best navigators of their time, had been in the service of the Portuguese government. They had found anew those long-lost sunset Islands of the Blest, now known as the Madeira and Canary Islands. Genoese sailors had even discovered the Azores, a thousand miles to the westward, half way across the broad Atlantic. Down the western coast of Africa had pushed those bold pilots from Genoa in the service of the most western State in continental Europe. Already in the thirteenth century Portuguese expeditions had passed Cape Non, a promontory so dangerous to navigators that men used grimly to say, "Whoever passes Cape Non will return or *not*." In 1435 Cape Bojador was doubled, and thus headland after headland was conquered as Portuguese discovery crept past Cape Blanco, Cape Verde and ever southwards to the region of Sierra Leone, where Hanno, the Carthaginian, had seen negroes and gorillas two thousand years before. What motives lured men ever onward? Love of adventure, the hunt for gold, the trade in slaves and ivory. The Phoenicians, the Carthaginians, the Arabians, and the Moors had all been engaged in the business of slave dealing. The Mohammedans taught it to the Portuguese and they taught it to the English.

A noble, scientific example to Columbus was his early contemporary, Prince Henry, the navigator, who sought a new route to India by way of the west coast of Africa. He had established a naval observatory at Sagres, the land's end of Portugal, the Sacred Promontory of the ancients, who supposed it to be the point farthest west on the habitable earth. There Prince Henry founded not only an observatory, but a school of geography. Thither like sea-gulls around a light-house flocked scholars, teachers, map-makers, and adventurous mariners. There, says John Fiske in his Discovery of America, I, 319, Prince Henry "spent the greater part of his life; thence he sent forth his captains to plough the southern seas; and as year after year the weather-beaten ships returned from their venturesome pilgrimage, the first glimpse of home that greeted them was likely to be the beacon-light in the tower where the master sat poring over problems of Archimedes or watching the stars."

Was there ever such a seminary for the training of geographers and discoverers of new lands? Prince Henry died in 1463, nine years before Columbus came to Portugal, but that scientific and adventurous spirit lived on in Lisbon, which was now the centre of geographical science. Bartholomew, the brother of Columbus, was already established there as a maker and publisher of maps recording Portuguese discoveries. Columbus himself was skilled in this art. He once said, "God gave me ingenuity and skill in designing charts and inscribing upon them, in the proper places, cities, rivers, mountains, isles, and ports." Indeed, he joined in many of those Portuguese maritime expeditions, and speaks of voyages to Guinea. Shortly before Columbus came to Lisbon, two Portuguese noblemen, Santaren and Escobar, had sailed down the Gold Coast and crossed the equator. Thence the land was found to bear away southwards. The Portuguese began to despair of ever doubling the continent of Africa and of reaching India by an eastern route.

Just here the grand idea of Columbus, of Cardinal D'Ailly, of Roger Bacon, and of Aristotle sprang into new life. It became clear to the Genoese pilot that the problem of a quick route to India was to be solved not by further and interminable groping down the African coast, but by boldly sailing westward around the globe. In 1474 the King of Portugal sought the advice of Paul Toscanelli, the great physicist in the republic of Florence, concerning a possible route to India. Shortly afterwards Columbus appealed to the same authority, and Toscanelli's answer is preserved. It is a clear and scientific statement of the whole case:

"Paul, the physicist, to Christopher Columbus, greeting. I perceive your great and noble desire to go to the place where the spices grow; wherefore in reply to a letter of yours, I send you a copy of another letter, which I wrote some time ago to a friend of mine, a gentleman of the household of the most gracious King of Portugal, . . . in reply to another, which by command of His Highness he wrote me concerning that matter: and I send you another sailing chart, similar to the one I sent him, by which your demands will be satisfied. The copy of that letter of mine is as follows:

" Paul, the physicist, to Fernando Martinez, canon, at Lisbon, greeting. . . . I have formerly spoken with you about a shorter route to the places of Spices by ocean navigation than that which you are pursuing by Guinea. The most gracious king now desires from me some statement, or rather an exhibition to the eye, so that even slightly educated persons can grasp and comprehend that route. Although I am well aware that this can be proved from the spherical shape of the earth, nevertheless, in order to make the point clearer and to facilitate the enterprise, I have decided to exhibit that route by means of a sailing chart. I therefore send to his majesty a chart made by my own hands, upon which are laid down your coasts, and the islands from which you must begin to shape your course steadily westward, and the places at which you are bound to arrive, and how far from the pole or from the equator you ought to keep away. . . . Do not wonder at my calling *west* the parts where the spices are, whereas they are commonly called *east*, because to persons sailing persistently westward those parts will be found by courses on the under side of the earth."[1]

Toscanelli's letter gives an elaborate and glowing description of the wealth of Cathay, the populous country of the Great Khan or King of Kings. "This country is worth seeking by the Latins, not only because great treasures may be obtained from it,—gold, silver, and all sorts of jewels and spices,—but on account of its learned men, philosophers and skilled astrologers." Toscanelli like Solomon was loyal to science and thus associated wisdom with rubies. He also expressed a commendable modern interest in the politics and administration of the country of Great Khan. In conclusion the Florentine professor of physics took special pains to inform Columbus that Lisbon was about 6,500 miles from "the great and splendid city of Quinsay," the Chinese King-see or Peking. From the island of Antilia to "the very splendid island of Cipango" it was only 2,500 miles. Toscanelli, following Marco Polo, said that island abounded " in gold, pearls, and precious stones, and they cover the temples and palaces with solid gold."

Marco Polo has been called "the true predecessor of Columbus." Polo spent seventeen years in China and was familiar with the geographical character of the Orient. He had been in the civil and diplomatic service of the Great Khan, whom he represented as the emperor of the far East. Upon his return to Europe Marco Polo gave a brilliant description of

---

[1] John Fiske, *Discovery of America*, Vol. I, p. 356.

the wealth of Cathay and especially of Zipango or Japan. Columbus became familiar with the writings of the Venetian traveller and it was the main object of the Genoese to reach the land of pearls and spices, the great archipelago comprising thousands of islands off the southeast coast of Asia.

Here we are at the bottom of the whole matter as it lay in the mind of Columbus. Away with idle talk about Vineland and the Norse Sagas, legends of northern discovery revived centuries after this era of Columbus. Although he did visit Iceland in 1477 he was now bent upon the discovery of the Zipango of Marco Polo and of more distant Cathay by a westward route according to the map and instructions of Toscanelli. That the Genoese pilot clearly apprehended the ideas of the Florentine physicist is perfectly apparent from another letter written by Toscanelli to Columbus. One extract tells us the whole story: "I regard as noble and grand your project of sailing from east to west according to the indications furnished by the map which I sent you, and which would appear still more plainly upon a sphere. I am much pleased to see that I have been well understood, and that the voyage has become not only possible but certain, fraught with honor as it must be and inestimable gain, and most lofty fame among all Christian people." The Italian physicist died in 1482, ten years before America was discovered.

Columbus first brought his project to the attention of King John of Portugal. It was by him referred to a joint commission of learned men and ecclesiastics, who declared that the scheme was altogether visionary and impracticable. The King's confessor, however, advised that the theory of Columbus be tested by a secret expedition. His charts were borrowed and the voyage was actually attempted, but it failed on account of the cowardice of the crew, who were beaten back by Atlantic storms. Columbus then went in disgust, and in some pecuniary embarrassment, to Spain in the year 1484 and there spent eight years in diligent propaganda of his noble scientific faith. It was condemned as heresy by narrow-

minded men, who said there could not be any antipodes, or
human beings on the other side of the world; for all men
were descended from Adam and the known world had already
been divided among his descendants. Moreover, if Columbus
and his ships should sail down the watery slope towards the
west, they could never get back again; it would be like sailing up a mountain. With such learned arguments did the
wise men of Spain oppose the grand project of Columbus.
But he made a few good friends among the more intelligent
clergy. Most helpful of all during this long and discouraging
period of neglect was Juan Perez, prior of the monastery at
La Rabida, near Palos, where Columbus left his son Diego to
be educated. "Let hatred and envy know," says Castelar,
the Spanish statesman, "that the humble Franciscan monk,
Juan Perez, in truth discovered the New World, through his
deep friendship and admiration for Columbus." There was a
women at court, the Marchioness de Moya, who befriended
Columbus; and there was also a keen-witted Italian churchman, Geraldini, who said one day to Cardinal Mendoza, the
Queen's confessor: "Good theologians are these critics of
Columbus, but mighty poor cosmographers."

Into the wanderings of the Spanish court from city to city,
into the long story of patient waiting and fruitless appeals for
government-aid we need not enter here. The final triumph
is closely associated with the surrender of the Alhambra and
the Moorish capital by Boabdil to Ferdinand and Isabella.
For more than seven hundred years the Christian powers of
Spain had been struggling with the Moslem. Granada was
the last stronghold of the infidel. For seven centuries Spain
had held back the tide of Mohammedan invasion pouring in
from the two continents of Africa and Asia. With this flood
forever turned away from Western Europe, Spain was now
ready to undertake the heroic enterprise of Columbus, to conquer and people a western world. Rather than to suffer rival
France to profit by his scheme, the Spanish government
appointed Columbus admiral, viceroy, governor-general of all

islands and territories that he might discover beyond the seas. Money for the expedition came not from the sale of the Queen's jewels, as is commonly said, but from her husband's cash-box, on his wife's promise to repay. Ferdinand had been confiscating Jewish property in Aragon and expelling Israelites from the kingdom. Not jewels but Jews were the real financial basis of the first expedition of Columbus. The entire outfit cost about $100,000.

The Jews were expelled from Spain August 2, 1492. On the very next day Columbus sailed from Palos, with three vessels and men numbering in all about one hundred and twenty. Among them there was of course a clever Jewish interpreter who could speak Arabic, Coptic, Armenian, and other oriental languages. Columbus carried a Latin letter of introduction from Ferdinand and Isabella to the Great Khan. An historian went with the expedition to record the truth, a notary to draft treaties and attach all movable property in the West; a physician and a metallurgist were also on board. Curiously enough there sailed peaceably together on this first voyage to the New World an Irishman and an Englishman. The little fleet was detained at the Canary Islands until the sixth of September, when the admiral put out to sea from the harbor of Gomera and sailed west for nearly five weeks.

> "Behind him lay the gray Azores,
>   Behind the gates of Hercules;
> Before him not the ghost of shores;
>   Before him only shoreless seas.
> The good mate said: 'Now must we pray,
>   For lo! the very stars are gone.
> Speak, admiral! what shall I say?'
>   Why, say 'sail on! sail on! and on!'"

The great poets are after all the best historians. Antiquarians and critics sometimes grope blindly for the sunshine of truth in the wilderness of trees, through swamps and tangled undergrowth, while poets remain upon the hill-tops in the sunlit open under the full-orbed day, and look out over forest and fen to the sparkling sea. I have read many accounts of Columbus' first great voyage of discovery, but nowhere have I found so much of the real meaning of that world-historic event as in the Psalm of the West, by our own Baltimore and University poet, Sidney Lanier. The heroic spirit of Columbus speaks through these lines and the spirit giveth light:

> "Ere we Gomera cleared, a coward cried,
>   *Turn, turn: here be three caravels ahead,*
>   *From Portugal, to take us: we are dead!*
> Hold Westward, pilot, calmly I replied.
> So when the last land down the horizon died,
>   *Go back, go back! they prayed: our hearts are lead.—*
>   Friends, we are bound into the West, I said.
> Then passed the wreck of a mast upon our side.
>   *See (so they wept) God's Warning! Admiral, turn!—*
>   Steersman, I said, hold straight into the West.
> Then down the night we saw the meteor burn.
>   *So do the very heavens in fire protest:*
>   *Good Admiral, put about! O Spain, dear Spain!—*
> Hold straight into the West, I said again.

> "Next drive we o'er the slimy-weeded sea.
>   *Lo! herebeneath (another coward cries)*
>   *The cursèd land of sunk Atlantis lies:*
> *This slime will suck us down—turn while thou'rt free!—*
> But no! I said, Freedom bears West for me!
> Yet when the long-time stagnant winds arise,
> And day by day the keel to westward flies,
> My Good my people's Ill doth come to be:
>   *Ever the winds into the West do blow;*
>   *Never a ship, once turned, might homeward go;*
>   Meanwhile we speed into the lonesome main.
>   *For Christ's sake, parley, Admiral! Turn, before*
>   *We sail outside all bounds of help from pain!—*
> Our help is in the West, I said once more.
>   *   *   *   *   *   *

> "I marvel how mine eye, ranging the Night,
>   From its big circling ever absently
>   Returns, thou large low Star, to fix on thee.
> Maria! Star? No star: a Light, a Light!
> Wouldst leap ashore, Heart? Yonder burns—a Light.

> Pedro Gutierrez, wake! come up to me.
> I prithee stand and gaze about the sea:
> What seest? *Admiral, like as land—a Light!*
> Well! Sanchez of Segovia, come and try:
> What seest? *Admiral, naught but sea and sky!*
> Well! But *I* saw it. Wait! the Pinta's gun!
> Why, look, 'tis dawn, the land is clear: 'tis done!
> Two dawns do break at once from Time's full hand—
> God's, East—mine, West: good friends, behold my Land!"

An island was first seen in the moonlight at a distance of about six miles by a common sailor named Rodrigo de Triana, on board the Pinta, at about two o'clock in the morning. The journal of Columbus records that he himself and Pedro Gutierrez had seen the light moving up and down like a candle at about ten o'clock in the evening. Justin Winsor, in his recent work on Columbus (p. 510), maintains that he could not have seen a light, for if it had been ahead the discoverers would have stopped; if it had been abeam they would not have left it. According to the log-book of Columbus, he sailed straight on for four hours at the rate of twelve miles an hour. This was apparently reckless navigation for an experienced admiral who had seen a light off shore or on shore.

The apparent difficulty is solved by a theory of Rudolf Cronau, the latest German authority upon the landfall of Columbus. Cronau thinks that the three caravels sailed past the light and the island on the north or south side and in the morning found themselves on the west or lee side of Watling's Island, where they landed in a safe harbor now known as Riding Rocks. With a strong wind blowing from the east Columbus would not have dared to land anywhere except on the leeward side. The physical geography of Watling's Island has served to identify the landfall of Columbus and at the same time enables us to believe with Cronau that the watchful admiral may indeed have seen the moving light on the east side four hours before the sailor Roderigo discovered land on the west side. At any rate it was characteristic that the first enterprising American should have gone west for some distance before disembarking.

Columbus afterwards claimed and received the reward offered by the King and Queen for the discovery, because he had first seen the light. The poor sailor Roderigo de Triana thought himself wronged, and after his return to Spain he is said to have renounced Christianity and to have made his abode with the Mohammedans, " whom he regarded as a juster people." All of which goes to show what a faithful, honest soul Roderigo possessed and how high he valued his soul and his religion in comparison with a pension for the discovery of a new world.

In the Boston Public Library there is the Roman edition, the *editio princeps* of the first letter [1] of Columbus on his return to Spain, announcing the discovery of America. It is reproduced in fac-simile by the heliotype process in the Bulletin of the Library for October, 1890. It is the rarest work in American history, of which it is the true beginning. The following extract is from the translation by R. H. Major, editor of the *Select Letters of Columbus* (London, 1847, Publications of the Hakluyt Society). The letter is addressed to the lord of the treasury, Raphael Sanchez:

" Thirty-three days after my departure from Cadiz I reached the Indian Sea, where I discovered many islands, thickly peopled, of which I took possession without resistance in the name of our most illustrious Monarch, by public proclamation and with unfurled banners. To the first of these islands, which is called by the Indians Guanahani, I gave the name of the blessed Savior (San Salvador), relying upon whose protection I had reached this as well as the other islands; to each

---

[1] A fac-simile of the letter in Spanish of Christopher Columbus, written on his return from his first voyage and addressed to Luis de Sant Angel, 15 Feb.-14 March, 1493, announcing the discovery of the New World, was issued in 1889 by Ellis & Elvey, 29 New Bond Street, London, from a unique copy in the possession of Mr. Brayton Ives, of New York.

of these I also gave a name." Then follows a careful and most interesting description of the first expedition.

Columbus thought he had discovered certain islands lying off the eastern coast of Asia not far from Japan. He had no idea that he had approached an entirely new continent. " His discovery," says Mr. Winsor, "was a blunder; his blunder was a new world; the new world is his monument!" Harrisse, the best American authority upon Columbus, takes a liberal view of this historic blunder, which opened the way to the real truth regarding America. Harrisse likens the discovery by Columbus to the first detection of the planet Neptune by Le Verrier, the astronomer who announced that certain irregularities in the motion of Uranus were due to disturbing influences by some unknown body in the heavens. By following his suggestions, skilled observers found a new planet on the first of January 1847, and yet many of Le Verrier's original computations were found to be erroneous. So it was with the geographical calculations of Columbus. He had supposed that Japan was only about twenty-five hundred miles distant from the Canaries. Even Toscanelli, the great physicist of Italy, had blundered in extending Asia eastward upon his map by nearly the entire width of the Pacific Ocean, although he had calculated the earth's circumference within one hundred and twenty-four miles of the correct estimate.

If Columbus had known the true distance from the Canary Islands to Japan, probably he would never have dared to attempt a voyage of twelve thousand miles upon unknown seas. The historic blunder which he made was simply an historic necessity, like many other human mistakes in science and philosophy. The great contribution which Columbus made to human knowledge was that he demonstrated the existence of lands in the west, beyond the Atlantic Ocean and thus " linked forever the two worlds." Harrisse regards this discovery as the greatest in modern times. Alexander von Humboldt calls Columbus a giant standing on the confines between mediaeval and modern history and says "his existence marks one of the great epochs in the history of the world." Mr. Clements R. Markham maintains that all the discoveries made by other navigators, in the lifetime of Columbus, on the coasts of America, (except that of Cabral), were directly due to the first voyage of the admiral and should be classed as Columbian discoveries. Las Casas, a contemporary of Columbus, took the same historic view and said the admiral was the first to open the gates of ocean which had been closed for thousands of years. "It was he that put the thread into the hands of the rest by which they found the clue to more distant parts."

Modern critics of Columbus sometimes tell us that he began his maritime career as a pirate and a sea-rover. So did the Vikings of Scandinavia and the mariners of England. Spirits of the Danes and Norsemen! Shades of Drake and Hawkins! Who, if not pirates, were the original makers of Normandy and England? "Brave sea-captain," says Carlyle. "Norse sea-king—Columbus, my hero, royalest sea-king of all." Columbus, we are told, was a kidnapper and a slave-trader. So were all the great voyagers of his time. Even Prince Henry the Navigator supported his naval college at Sagres by the slave trade. Are we men of the nineteenth century so far removed from the treaty of Washington in 1842 which stopped the slave trade that we can talk reproachfully of it in the fifteenth century? Columbus, it is said, scornfully, was a seeker after gold.[1]

---

[1] We should not forget in the consideration of this gold-hunting spirit of Columbus, that he was driven on not only by the spirit of his time but by a natural desire to pay the expenses of his expedition and to satisfy the insatiable greed of his sovereign patrons. Personally he had a large ambition to use the spoil of the new world for the purpose of a new crusade. Savonarola and Columbus were in spirit among the last of the crusaders. The inroads of the Turks and the capture of Constantinople in 1453 inflamed mens' imaginations with schemes of oriental conquest and for the delivery of Jerusalem from the infidel. This crusading and religious spirit in Columbus was fostered by the long wars of Spain with the Mohammedans and by the final triumph of Ferdinand and Isabella over the Moorish kingdom of Granada in 1492.

What have men been doing since the beginning of the world or even since the Argonauts sailed westward to California in 1849? The poor Genoese pilot was ambitious. Ah, yes! Men do say that Caesar was ambitious. Columbus wanted, not a crown, but a vice-royalty in his island realm. What a craven he would have been, with his royal soul, to have accepted less power and honor than was accorded to Spanish admirals of his time.[1]

"I ought to be judged," said Columbus in one of his later letters, "as a captain sent from Spain to the Indies, to conquer a nation numerous and warlike, with customs and religion altogether different to ours; a people who dwell in the mountains, without regular habitations for themselves or for us; and where, by the Divine will, I have subdued another world to the dominion of the King and Queen, our sovereigns; in consequence of which, Spain, that used to be called poor, is

---

[1] In the prerogatives granted to Christopher Columbus by the King and Queen of Spain, at Granada, April 30, 1492, he was given the powers of viceroy and governor over the new lands that he might discover: "For as much as you, Christopher Columbus, are going by our command, with some of our vessels and men, to discover and subdue some Islands and Continent in the ocean, and it is hoped that by God's assistance, some of the said Islands and Continent in the ocean will be discovered and conquered by your means and conduct, therefore it is but just and reasonable, that since you expose yourself to such danger to serve us, you should be rewarded for it. And we being willing to honour and favour you for the reasons aforesaid; Our will is, That you, Christopher Columbus, after discovering and conquering the said Islands and Continent in the said ocean, or any of them, shall be our Admiral of the said Islands and Continent you shall so discover and conquer; and that you be our Admiral, Vice-Roy, and Governour in them, and that for the future, you may call and style yourself, D. Christopher Columbus, and that your sons and successors in the said employment, may call themselves Dons, Admirals, Vice-Roys, and Governours of them; and that you may exercise the office of Admiral, with the charge of Vice-Roy and Governour of the said Islands and Continent, which you and your Lieutenants shall conquer, and freely decide all causes, civil and criminal, appertaining to the said employment of Admiral, Vice-Roy, and Governour, as you shall think fit in justice, and as the Admirals of our kingdoms use to do."— *Charters and Constitutions of the U. S.*, Part I., p. 304.

now the most wealthy of kingdoms. I ought to be judged as a captain, who for so many years has borne arms, never quitting them for an instant. I ought to be judged by cavaliers who have themselves won the meed of victory; by knights of the sword and not of title deeds; as least, so it would have been among the Greeks and Romans, or any modern nation in which exists so much nobility as in Spain." [1]

Something of the haughty spirit of Cortes and Pizarro was in this Columbus of ours. By all accounts he was noble and even kingly in his appearance. He could not be false to his royal nature. Columbus is blamed for cruelty to his men. A commanding officer must sometimes be cruel in dealing with cut-throats, pirates, and mutineers. Columbus, we are told, did not succeed in ruling his colony and in preserving order. Possibly he was not cruel enough. Indeed Columbus was far too good a man for the company he kept and for the King he served. Columbus was loyal to his own standards of duty to church and State; but Ferdinand, the king who had proved false to both Moors and Jews, thought nothing of breaking his promise to Columbus. At the end of his third voyage he was superseded in office and was sent home to Spain a royal captive.

Tarducci [2] says of Columbus, "the chains in which he had been brought home as a prisoner from the New World, and which he had always kept hung up in his room as a memorial of the reward bestowed for his services, he directed to be placed in his sepulcher after his death; and his will was in this respect punctually executed. No one seemed aware of his passing away. The death of the discoverer of the New World [in 1506 at the age of fifty-nine] [3] passed without notice within the walls of the city [Valladolid] where he died. . . .

---

[1] *Select Letters of Columbus*, pp. 169-170.

[2] Tarducci's *Life of Columbus*, p. 365.

[3] Mr. Clements R. Markham has determined by various lines of historical argument, that 1447 was the year of the birth of Columbus.

But the oblivion with which the malice of his enemies succeeded in surrounding his person was soon dispelled by the brilliant splendor of his fame, to which time gave ever-increasing strength and vigor. . . . King Ferdinand was forced to yield to the growing influence, and ordered a monument erected to the man he had caused to expire in poverty and anguish in a lodging house."[1]

The world has gone on building monuments and erecting statues in honor of Christopher Columbus. The popular heart beats truer than the pulse of princes or detractors. The fame of Columbus has been slowly maturing through the centuries, but it has blossomed gloriously after four hundred years. In 1792 Baltimore was the only American city possessing a monument in honor of the discoverer of the New World. This monument now stands on the grounds of the Samuel Ready Asylum, between North Avenue and the Harford Road. It is an obelisk, forty-four feet and four inches high. The base is six and a half feet square; the top is about two and a half feet square. The monument is made of brick and mortar, stuccoed or cemented on the outside so that it has the appearance of grey sandstone. Some of our resident Baltimoreans are not quite sure whether this modest shaft was not erected by Zenos Barnum in memory of a favorite horse;[2] but

---

[1] The low state to which Columbus was reduced at the time of his fourth voyage to America is described in the following extract from his letter to the King and Queen of Spain : " Such is my fate, that the twenty years of service through which I have passed with so much toil and danger, have profited me nothing, and at this very day I do not possess a roof in Spain that I can call my own; if I wish to eat or sleep, I have nowhere to go but to the inn or tavern, and most times lack wherewith to pay the bill. Another anxiety wrung my very heartstrings, which was the thought of my son Diego, whom I had left an orphan in Spain, and stripped of the honour and property which were due to him on my account, although I had looked upon it as a certainty, that your Majesties, as just and grateful Princes, would restore it to him in all respects with increase." (*Select Letters of Christopher Columbus*, p. 179).

[2] The origin of this extraordinary tradition, in which many honest people continue to believe, is possibly due to a popular confusion of the Columbus

others who are better informed indignantly reject such a shallow and vulgar tradition. The balance of probability is overwhelmingly against the notion of a horse named "Christopher Columbus" dying on the 12th of October, 1792, on the three hundredth anniversary of the discovery of America. The inscription on the west side of this monument is engraved upon a marble slab and reads as follows:

SACRED
TO THE
MEMORY
OF
CHRIS
COLUMBUS
Octob. XII
MDCCVIIIC.

The Roman numerals VIII are placed before the final C to indicate that they are to be subtracted from one hundred, thus leaving the date 1792. This archaic inscription is ot itself sufficient evidence of the honest and historic purpose of the man who erected the monument. The managers of the Samuel Ready Asylum have a record of the ownership of their estate which has been traced back through Baltimore land records as far as 1787. In 1789 the property came into the possession of a Frenchman named Charles Francis Adrian le Paulmier Chevalier d'Anmour. To some critics and scoffers the unconscionable length of this name and a popular corruption of it into the form of *D'Amour* have made it seem fictitious, but the Chevalier D'Anmour was an historic character, who ought never to have been forgotten in our local history. He was the first French consul in Baltimore. He

---

monument with the Wilkens monument to a horse, in the western neighborhood of Baltimore on the Frederick road. This latter monument is, however, very modern.

is mentioned in the Journals of Congress as far back as October 27, 1778, soon after our first treaty with France. He was the first appointed consul in the State of Maryland, with a commission from Gérard, minister plenipotentiary and consul-general. In 1779 and 1780 D'Anmour's commission was extended to Virginia and North Carolina. In 1783 the Chevalier became consul-general of France for the State of Maryland, the Commonwealth of Virginia, and the States of North Carolina, South Carolina, and Georgia (See Journals of Congress, vol. III., 102, 330, 427; vol. IV., 263). In the Maryland Journal and Baltimore Advertiser of December 17, 1782, the following marriage is recorded : " The Honourable Le Chevalier D'Anmour, His Most Christian Majesty's Consul for the Middle District of the United States, to Miss Julia De Rocour, a young Lady lately arrived here from the West Indies." In the Journals of Congress the name is spelled in various ways,—D'Anemours, D'Annemours, and D'Anmour. The latter appears to be the phonetic form into which the original name was finally reduced.

It is clear from the land records of Baltimore that the Chevalier D'Anmour owned the estate upon which the Columbus monument, bearing the date 1792, now stands. The French consul acquired the property in 1789 and held it until 1796, when it passed into the hands of Archibald Campbell. In the library of the Maryland Historical Society there may be seen by any visitor a framed map of Baltimore, printed in 1801, showing the Campbell estate and upon it a picture of the monument in question. This simple fact ought to discredit forever the absurd popular tradition of a monument "*Sacred to the Memory*" of Zenos Barnum's horse. The Campbell estate did not come into the possession of the Barnum family until the year 1833—more than forty years after the Columbus monument was erected. The inscription October 12, 1792, upon a monument erected upon D'Anmour's own land and near his own house, ought to be taken at its face value as demonstrating the historic commemoration, by the generous and public spirited Chevalier, of the tercentenary of the discovery of America. The very existence of the monument with its marble tablet and historic inscription, proves that its founder was an admirer of Columbus and a friend of the land potentially discovered on that historic day, October 12, three centuries before. The important point which now remains for Baltimoreans to establish is this: their Columbus monument is probably the oldest[1] in the New World in honor of its discoverer.

Next to Baltimore comes Washington in point of priority in doing honor to Columbus in North America. The east

---

[1] In the appendix to this address Mr. Charles W. Bump, a graduate student of the Johns Hopkins University, has prepared a list of the various monuments to Columbus, with the aid of Mr. Frederick A. Ober, recently of the Latin American Department of the World's Columbian Exposition and special commissioner of the West Indies. From this list it will appear that the Baltimore monument to Columbus antedates the Havana monument by three years.

The existence of this Baltimore monument in memory of Columbus was first made known to Johns Hopkinsians in 1876, the opening year of the University, by its first librarian, Arthur Wellington Tyler, who in company with the present librarian, Mr. N. Murray, and his brother, Professor T. C. Murray, chanced one day while walking in the country to find this curious obelisk of brick and stucco in a grove of cedar trees, near the remains of some rude earth-works that had been hastily thrown up for the defence of Baltimore in the time of the late civil war. In 1876, North Avenue had not yet been opened and the monument stood at some distance from the nearest thoroughfare. The writer well remembers the mild excitement produced in a small academic circle by the startling announcement made by Mr. Tyler of his discovery of a monument to Christopher Columbus in the neighborhood of Baltimore. The historical department went out in a body of one, with the original discoverers, to see the obelisk and its remarkable inscription. It was the first archaeological discovery by Johns Hopkinsians and it created an historical enthusiasm akin to that of the Pickwick Club, when its founder discovered a Roman inscription, which, however, some skeptics interpreted as "Bil Stumps His Mark." Our ardor for Columbian inscriptions was somewhat dampened when we were told by native Baltimoreans that the "Chris Columbus" monument was erected in memory of a horse bearing that historic name. But to this day some of us have continued in our original faith and have steadfastly maintained that a

portico of the Capitol has broad stone steps flanked by large buttresses. On the south buttress there is a large marble group representing the discovery of America. It was executed by an Italian sculptor named Persico in 1846 at a cost of $40,000. Columbus is represented holding aloft a small globe inscribed " America," while at his side crouches an Indian maiden. The figure of Columbus is encased in armor. The bronze door, called the "Columbus Door" at the main entrance to the Capitol, was modelled at Rome in 1858 by Randolph Rogers, the American sculptor, and was cast in Munich in 1860. It is nineteen feet in height and nine feet wide. It weighs 20,000 pounds and cost $28,000. On it are designs

---

monument, bearing the inscription "Sacred to the Memory of Christopher Columbus, October 12, 1792" must be the memorial of a man and not of a beast, of an historic event and not of an equine death and burial.

The subject was first carefully investigated by a writer for the Baltimore *American*, November 19, 1880. The opening of Boundary Avenue had brought the old-time monument within plain view of passers-by. The contributor to *The American*, although born and reared within half a mile of the spot, said that he had never known, until three months before, of the existence of the monument. He proceeded to describe its location and appearance: " On the east side of the Harford turnpike, leading out of Baltimore City, adjoining what has for several years past been known as ' Darley Park,' about one and a half miles from the City Hall, has stood for a century past an old-fashioned, substantial and spacious mansion house, with numerous outbuildings, all of stone and old English brick. It is just discernible through the branches of numerous aged trees, at a distance of perhaps three hundred yards from the road. For half a century it has been known as the Barnum property, having been, and still being, in the possession of the family of that name, who were the founders of the famous Barnum's Hotel. Thirty or forty years ago the elder David Barnum resided here. The tract comprises about twenty-five acres, and the grounds around the old mansion house, although sadly out of repair since the death of David Barnum some twenty years ago, are still inviting and picturesque, with their box-wood walks, bordered roadways lined with rows of cedars, fine old fruit trees, and rosebush clusters here and there. In the rear, southeast corner of the enclosure stands the Columbus Monument, on an elevated plateau, which seems to have been artificially arranged."

The reporter then gave the legendary accounts of the monument, with various popular stories all manifestly inventions and absolutely untrust-

in high relief illustrative of the career of Columbus. The casing is covered with emblematic designs and on the top of the arch is a bust of Columbus. There are eight panels on the door and also a transom panel. On them the following scenes represent to the eye the life of our hero : the examination of Columbus before the Council of Salamanca; departure of Columbus from the convent of La Rabida for the Spanish Court; Columbus before the court of Ferdinand and Isabella; departure of Columbus from Palos on his first voyage of discovery; Columbus landing at San Salvador; first encounter of Columbus with the Indians; triumphal entrance of Co-

---

worthy; but, at the same time, he gave the correct and historic view, that the shaft was erected by the first French consul in Maryland, who had bought the estate upon which the monument now stands. "Early in the present century," the writer continues, "the property was owned by Thomas Tenant, a wealthy, influential and a leading citizen of Baltimore. One of his daughters, became the wife of Hon. John P. Kennedy. Another daughter is now living at an advanced age, in New York City, and only two years since paid a visit to the old homestead and sat beneath the shadow of the Columbus monument. She stated that it stood in her early childhood just as it stands now, and was often visited by noted Italians and Frenchmen, who seemed to know of it in Europe."

The subject of the Columbus monument was investigated anew by an undergraduate student of the Johns Hopkins University, Mr. Victor Rosewater, son of the editor of *The Omaha Bee*, which first published the young writer's results. They were afterward revised by him in New York and were republished in *Frank Leslie's Illustrated Weekly*, December 20, 1890. Rosewater's original article was accepted by Mr. William E. Curtis, of the Bureau of American Republics, and became the basis of an official account of the Baltimore monument and also of his recent article on "Columbus monuments," in *The Chautauquan* for November, 1892. Another article on the Baltimore monument to Columbus appeared in the *Baltimore American*, August 4, 1891.

The present writer is greatly indebted to Mr. Henry F. Thompson, of the Maryland Historical Society, for valuable information and references confirming the above historic view of the Columbus monument. Mr. Thompson lived in its immediate vicinity in his early life and is perfectly confident, from his own family traditions, that the shaft was erected in memory of the discoverer of America.

36   *Columbus and his Discovery of America.*

lumbus into Barcelona; Columbus in chains; death bed of
Columbus.

In the National Museum at Washington there is a most
interesting relic of Columbus, namely a piece of the bolt to
which he was chained in the fortress at San Domingo. There
is also to be seen in the National Museum an old door from
the convent at La Rabida at Palos, where Columbus found
shelter for himself and son with the good prior Juan Perez.
At the World's Fair in Chicago there will be exhibited a
magnificent collection of relics, photographs, and pictures
illustrating Columbus and his time.

Many cities now have a Columbus statue. The Italian
citizens of Baltimore have placed in our Druid Hill Park, a
statue of their great countryman, by Achille Canessa. Philadelphia has a Columbus statue in her Fairmount Park. In
New York, at the west entrance to Central Park, stands
the noblest statue of the noble Genoese pilot. It was presented to the people of this country by the Italians of the
United States, Canada, Mexico, and Central America. It is
of Carrara marble, and was modelled by Gaetano Russo, an
Italian sculptor in Rome. It is one of the finest works of
modern Italian art. This international monument, with its
granite base and column, stands seventy-five feet high. At
the base of the column there is a statue of the genius of Italy
bending over a globe and discovering a new continent. On
the opposite side there is a representation of the American
eagle holding the shields of Genoa and Spain. There are also
two bronze reliefs upon the base, one picturing Columbus and
his men when they first saw land and the other showing the
first landing. At Madrid there is a fine statue of Columbus
representing him in the solemn religious act of taking possession of the New World in the name of Christian Spain. He
stands looking steadfastly upward, with the flag of Spain in
his hand. In the city of Genoa there is the grandest monument in the world in honor of Columbus.

The various statues and portraits [1] of the great navigator have no uniform type; but what matters it whether we have the man's exact likeness in marble or on canvas? It is the ideal Columbus that the world wishes to commemorate. Purified and ennobled, his great soul has become again incarnate in the imagination of artists and of great peoples who unite to do him honor in this Columbian year.

Let no one regret that the New World was not named in honor of Columbus. As Pericles said of the Athenian generals slain : " The whole earth is the monument of illustrious men." The name "America" is a beautiful and worthy Germanic name meaning rich in industry, in active busy life. It was not an honor stolen from Columbus by Amerigo Vespucci, the Florentine, but it was bestowed by a German monk, Martin Waldseemüller, upon the land which Amerigo had so well described in his letters to the Medici. The motive was at once scientific and monkish. Europe, said Martin the geographer of the monastic college of San Dié, was named after a woman; let us have one continent named after a man.

The eternal womanly has risen triumphant and serene in "Columbia," the spirit of American liberty. It was no calamity for Columbus that he was prevented from becoming the viceroy, the Pizarro of the new world or from stamping his name upon a continent. In losing all, he gained all; and the Holy Mother Church will perhaps some day pronounce

---

[1] Pictures of some of the monuments and statues above mentioned and of certain portraits of Columbus were exhibited during the delivery of Dr. Adams' address. Among others was shown the Lotto portrait of Columbus, described by Mr. John C. Van Dyke in *The Century Magazine* for October, 1892.

In a recent address, October 26, before the Union League Club of Philadelphia, Mr. Chauncey M. Depew says that he met Columbus at the Chicago celebration and asked him if he was going to stay with us. "Well," he said, "after seeing about five hundred of my alleged portraits around this city, I have made up my mind to return."

him blessed. Happy already is this modern St. Christopher,[1] who brought the colonies of Christian Europe across the western sea.

One hundred years ago the discoverer of America was first publicly honored in this City of Baltimore. To-day we recall and apply to him the spirit of our own Baltimore motto, which by some curious historic chance has come down to us in the language of Italy and of Columbus. *Fatti maschii, parole femine*, manly deeds and womanly words, belong to the world-pilot of Genoa as well as to Lord Baltimore, the first great American apostle of tolerant opinion. The manliest deed in American history was that first great voyage of Columbus across an unknown, western sea. The generous and true-hearted words of our Baltimore poet have nobly characterized that great Italian who led the way to this larger world. The Psalm of the West by Sidney Lanier, the laureate of our University, who though dead will speak forevermore in words of music, is the noblest tribute to the historic memory of Christopher Columbus. We Hopkinsians honor the great Captain for his immortal deed, which first brought the old

---

[1] In connection with his book on *America; Its Geographical History*. (Extra Volume XIII of the Johns Hopkins University Studies.) Dr. Walter B. Scaife has brought out a fac-simile of the American portion of Juan de la Cosà's map of the world, 1500, representing also St. Christopher carrying the Christ-child across the sea. Mr. R. H. Major has used a chromolithograph of this picture as the frontispiece to his second edition (1870) of the *Select Letters of Columbus*. Mr. Major and others have suggested that St. Christopher represents Christopher Columbus carrying the Christian faith across the Atlantic, and that the face is a portrait. In corroboration of this idea, Mr. Major quotes Herrera's description: "Columbus was tall of stature, with a long and imposing visage. His nose was aquiline; his eyes blue; his complexion clear, and having a tendency to a glowing red; the beard and hair red in his youth, but his fatigues early turned them white." The late Henry Stevens once said that the Cosa map is the most precious cartographical document relating to the New World. This map was bought some years ago by the Queen of Spain and it is now in the Naval Museum at Madrid.

World into historical contact with the New. The light he saw—

> "It grew a starlit flag unfurled!
> It grew to be Time's burst of dawn.
> He gained a world; he gave that world
> Its grandest lesson: 'On and on!'"

What indomitable purpose was that of Columbus! It was steadily pursued through twenty years of ridicule, with at first only two men and two women who did not laugh at him,— Juan Perez the Franciscan, Diego Deza the Dominican, the Marchioness de Moya and Queen Isabella. Think of it! The organized forces of society, church, state, and university, all arrayed against him! But he mastered them all,—prelates, courtiers, and learned doctors of Spain. He conquered the prejudices of a thousand years and then died a martyr to his heroic cause. Christopher Columbus, the son of Italy, the heir of all the ages, he did this great and manly deed; he discovered a world. *He did it;* for that reason we honor him. He sacrificed all; and for this reason we love him.

"Men, my brothers, men the workers ever reaping something new;
That which they have done but earnest of the things which they shall do."

In the fields of science and religion, in art and letters, in civic and social reform, in the improvement of great peoples and in the elevation of mankind, there are still new worlds for discovery and conquest. The heavens above and the earth beneath and even the depths of the great sea are full of fresh materials for observation and research. The beauty of this rolling cosmos is that the infinitely small is as wonderful as the infinitely great. From the red planet Mars and the new moon of Jupiter to a microscopic germ of life or black death, the range of all scientific inquiry is equally noble and rewarding. Let us then, comrades all, press forward. As Aeneas said to his companions, "It is not too late to seek another world."

II.
THE DISCOVERY OF AMERICA.[1]

A new world discovered is a gift too large for anything less than the whole world to receive. Columbus thought to enrich Castile with the treasures of the Indies, and enriched Europe with treasures which beggared all Asia in comparison. He called every islet after the tutelary saints of Spain, and the continent they skirt was named by a German. He labored for his own age, and other centuries have entered into his labors. He sought an inheritance for the heirs of his body forever, and a people of sixty millions now invite his last descendant to come and pronounce that inheritance fair.

But the discoveries fraught with largest destinies to man have always found human agents, in some measure worthy of them. The deed that dwarfs the beholder looks with levelled eyes into the soul of the doer. The Columbus who died neglected in a Spanish inn, so forgotten already in life, that not one ear seems to have marked the bell that tolled the passage of his mounting spirit,—this man made no compromise with defeat. He was, in his forlorn death, as near the heart of his

---

[1] Oration by Professor Henry Wood, of the Johns Hopkins University, at the Columbus Celebration in Baltimore, October 21, 1892. The festival was arranged by four Baltimore singing societies, the Liederkranz, Arion, Germania Mænnerchor and Arbeiter Mænnerchor, for the production, on the four hundredth anniversary of the discovery of America, of the prize cantata "Columbus," composed by Mr. D. Melamet, a resident of Baltimore.

discovery as he had been in the flush of success. If he directed
that the chains in which he had been brought back to Spain
should be placed with him in his grave, some may find in the
words the expression of an exaggerated vanity, but this is the
language that the world loves to hear great men use. If he
thought he had been prophesied of in Holy Writ, as one that
should come, this is the form in which his intensely religious
age expressed the exalted mission of men who make history.
And when, on the eve of his first voyage across the Atlantic,
he dedicated the riches he expected to win to the rescue of the
Holy Sepulchre, he devoted the revenues of a world to the
service of the highest ideal he knew.

No serious writer has ever questioned Columbus' religious
sincerity. We may call it fanaticism, but is that any gain?
The first man who believed in America enough to go and find
it in the way Columbus did ought to be permitted by Americans to believe anything else he chooses. It is said that he
gained his religious fervor in Spain. There is something of
the mysticism of a Calderon in it, and it was a Duke of Veraguas—ancestor of the Duke lately invited to America as
Columbus' lineal representative—who, in 1680, was first
instrumental in collecting the works of Calderon for publication.

Whoever leaves this element out in estimating the character of Columbus, can never hope to understand him. And is
it so impossible to translate his fervid mysticism into the
language of to-day? Spain had fought the Moor for seven
hundred years at home, but Columbus was the first real
Spanish crusader, the first who in thought made Spain overleap her national boundaries and join hands with the rest of
Christian Europe in the realization of a universal idea. It
was not to be! Spain was not to rescue the Holy Sepulchre
from the Unbelievers, but Columbus was to wrest a continent
from the mysterious terrors of the Sea of Darkness. Spain
never rose to the height of a universal idea, not even in her
most splendid period. Columbus carried the idea with him

across the ocean; and that universal idea, translated into the language of our time, is America; not the America that is, but as we hope and believe it shall become. This discoverer partakes of the universal and unending nature of his discovery and shall grow with it. When I look at him—the bold dreamer of a sacred areopagus, seated in Jerusalem—and then turn to look at America, throned in the West, it but

"Drowns his dream in larger stream,
As morning drinks the morning star."

America, as a present great reality, is all around us, and eloquent apostles of this reality are not far to seek. But is America, as an idea, less real? To Columbus it was nothing more, and yet the country is honoring his memory as the memory of no other American has ever been honored. And to many since Columbus' time who never reached these shores America, while conveying a territorial and political notion, has conveyed an ideal notion, stronger if not more distinct—a widened horizon of thought and life, a hope, an inspiration. The inheritance of the American people in this country is inseparable from another privilege, another duty—the stewardship of a world-ideal!

The German author of the "Ship of Fools," writing in the year after the discovery of America, chronicles the opinion of the age then closing when he declares that "A wise man should stay at home: or, if he find himself by chance at sea, make for the shore as quickly as possible. The Eldorado is far off, and you are more likely to be drowned than to reach it. The man who travels cannot perfectly serve God." One hundred years later our English Elizabethan poet, Chapman, tells us what life meant to his age in a splendid tribute to the English voyagers to the mouths of the Orinoco, the very coast Columbus had finally reached. The title "Guiana" must be taken as typical of the American idea in his mind, and the whole poem is symbolical.

The Discovery of America. 43

"Oh, you patrician spirits, that refine
Your flesh to fire, and issue like a flame
On brave endeavors, knowing that in them
The tract of Heaven in morn-like glory opens,
You know that death lives where power lives unused!"

If we could dam in and utilize the current of inspiration which, in the idea America or suggested by it, foams and dashes through English Elizabethan literature and life, it would propel the mills of our national thought and action better than a harnessed Niagara can grind our corn. These men are like younger brethren of Columbus, voyaging across mysterious seas of thought and life. Columbus sailed for Asia, and found America. The Elizabethans sailed for the new Eldorado of the West, and found it in their own bosoms. It was there the Pilgrim Fathers found it, there Lord Baltimore, there a Penn, a Franklin; and every true American must find it there anew.

In the science of geometry a straight line marks the shortest distance between two given points. In the world's history a great deed, a great discovery, is the luminous straight line between great movements of the intellect. It cables the oceans and makes the centuries neighbors; it is the courier conveying messages between the kings of thought. The great deed of Columbus joins Aristotle with Roger Bacon and Humboldt. We saw it reaching back to the Crusades and forward to the English Renaissance. Permit me for a moment to trace it further forward to our own age—to Goethe.

In the midst of the French Revolution and with the American war of independence fresh in mind Goethe wrote the following words: "I will turn back, and in my own house, in my own garden, surrounded by my own friends, I will say, 'Here or nowhere is America!'"

And this is the man who wrote "Faust"! In Columbus' discovery a larger macrocosm is revealed—imago mundi; in "Faust" the attempt at a new microcosm—the imago hominis of the present age. The discovery of the new world by Columbus was the answer to the first ardent, longing question of the modern man, " Where shall I find room for the expansion of the new powers within me?" Goethe's " Faust " deals with the second no less momentous question, " In this chaos of unchartered freedom where shall I find and how shall I fulfil my duty to my fellow-man?" And the answer? We find it in the last words of the now chastened and purified but still titanic Faust :

> " To millions let me give a native soil,
> Though not secure, yet free to active toil ;
> Green, fertile fields, where men and herds go forth
> In peace and comfort, on the newest earth.
> A land like paradise here, round about :
> Up to the shore the tide may roar without,
> And though it gnaw, to burst with force the limit,
> By common impulse all unite to hem it.
> Yes! to this thought I hold with firm persistence ;
> The last result of wisdom stamps it true :
> He only earns his freedom and existence,
> Who daily conquers them anew.
> Thus here, by dangers girt, shall glide away
> Of childhood, manhood, age, the vigorous day ;
> And such a throng I fain would see,—
> Stand on free soil among a people free !"

Do we not recognize this picture? The creative answer of the German poet to the riddle of life, the new world descried from the sea of modern passion and doubt, is but another realization of the American idea. The achievement of Columbus becomes the duty of the present; the deed of the fifteenth century reappears as the prophecy of the nineteenth.

And this gift of a world to a world is ours! The dream of early sages, the longing of centuries, the manifest ordering of Divine Providence, the deed of Columbus; the overflowings of European manhood, the spirit of our forefathers, the hope of the republic, the proper study of every citizen !

Our inheritance is our opportunity.

III.

THE FIRST JEW IN AMERICA.

Upon the Exodus of the Jews from Spain, we should recall, in this Columbian year, the "Little Poems in Prose" by Emma Lazarus and her lines to the year "1492:"

"The Spanish noon is a blaze of azure fire, and the dusty pilgrims crawl like an endless serpent along treeless plains and bleached high-roads, through rock-split ravines and castellated, cathedral-shadowed towns.

"Whither shall they turn? for the West hath cast them out, and the East refuseth to receive.

"O bird of the air, whisper to the despairing exiles, that to-day, to-day, from the many-masted, gayly-bannered port of Palos, sails the world-unveiling Genoese, to unlock the golden gates of sunset and bequeath a Continent to Freedom!   *   *   *   *   *   *

"Unto her ample breast, the generous mother of nations welcomes them.

"The herdsman of Canaan and the seed of Jerusalem's royal shepherd renew their youth amid the pastoral plains of Texas and the golden valleys of the Sierras."

1492.

Thou two-faced year, Mother of Change and Fate,
Didst weep when Spain cast forth with flaming sword,
The children of the prophets of the Lord,
Prince, priest, and people, spurned by zealot hate.
Hounded from sea to sea, from state to state,
The West refused them, and the East abhorred.
No anchorage the known world could afford,
Close-locked was every port, barred every gate.
Then smiling, thou unveil'dst, O two-faced year,
A virgin world where doors of sunset part,
Saying, "Ho, all who weary, enter here!
There falls each ancient barrier that the art
Of race or creed or rank devised, to rear
Grim bulwarked hatred between heart and heart!"

The First Jew in America.

The following extract is from an article published in "The Menorah Monthly," Oct., 1892, by Dr. M. Kayserling, Professor in the Theological Seminary in Buda-Pesth. He is a leading authority upon the subject of the Jews in Spain. The close connection between the expulsion of that people and the sailing of Columbus from Spain was briefly noticed in the address by Mr. Adams at the Peabody Institute, *ante* p. 20. Professor Kayserling calls attention to the same point and to some interesting facts regarding the first "wandering Jew" who discovered and explored the New World.

"In the same month in which their Majesties issued the edict that all Jews should be driven out of the kingdom and the territories, in the same month they gave me the order to undertake, with sufficient men, my expedition of discovery to the Indies." With these words Cristobal Colon as the Spaniards call him, commenced the diary, which he kept. With the same pen with which the royal couple of Spain signed the glorious capitulation of Granada, with the same pen they signed the disastrous edict of the expulsion of the Jews and the contract they concluded after long hesitation with the Genoese sailor.

The discovery of the world stands in close relation with the expulsion of the Jews, not only as to time, but as to its whole nature. On the 2nd of August, on the 9th day of the Jewish month of the Ab, the national day of sorrow for the twice-occurring destruction of the capital of the Jewish State, half a million of Jews left their Spanish home. The day thereafter, on Friday, the 3rd day of August, Columbus sailed away to find the sea-passage to India, to discover a new world. He was accompanied by one hundred and twenty, according to others by only ninety, men all natives of Castile and Aragon, Avila, Segovia, Guadalajara, Caceres, Castrajeriz, Villar Talavera, all of them places where small Jewish congregations existed until the expulsion.

Were there in the Armada, which under Columbus sailed toward a new world, also men belonging to the Jewish race? Columbus had by no means an easy task to find men to join him on his adventurous expedition, so that even convicts could obtain pardon by declaring their readiness to enlist. What should have prevented homeless persecuted Jews to take part in the expedition? Sailors were found among the Jews long before Columbus's time. Why, to cite only one instance, a certain Joseph Faquin, of Barcelona, sailed over the "whole world," as testified to by King Jaime of Aragon.

After a long sail, full of danger, a glimmer of light became visible in the distance and on the morning of the 12th of October, on the day on which the Jews sang in their synagogues their Hosanna, a voice announced to the sailors, "Tierra! Tierra!" Who was the first that beheld the land? It is not a sportive question. The royal couple of Spain had assured to him, who should first see an island of the new world, an annual pension of ten thousand maravedis.

The Chronicler Gonçalo Hernandez de Oviedo, a contemporary of Columbus, said he had been informed by Vicente Yanéz Pinzon, the commander of the "Nina," one of the three ships which composed the first fleet, and from the pilot, Hernao Perez Matheos, that it was a man of Lepe who had first seen and exclaimed "Land." But as Columbus in his greed refused to concede to him the reward, and rather kept it for himself, that sailor took his leave, went to Africa and there changed from Christianity to his former creed. Was that Judaism? The Chronicler[1] is silent on that subject: he who prides himself of having seen the exodus of the Jews from Spain and to have heard their loud wails. According to others it was Rodrigo de Triana who saw land first, the Watlings or Acklin Islands, which the natives called Guanahani. . . .

A man of the Jewish race was the first who, next to Rodrigo Triana, saw land. It was Rodrigo Sanchez, a relative of

---

[1] Coronica de las Indias (1547), Cap. 5, Pag. 7a; . . . porque no se le dieron las albrécias . . . se pusso en Affricay renego la fé. Gomara, Historia de las Indias, P. 168: i asi, el marinér de Lepe se pasó se Berberia y allo renegó la fe.

the royal treasurer, Gabriel Sanchez, who accompanied the first expedition at the request of Queen Isabella, as "veedor," or superintendent.

We do not speak at this time of a few other men who took part in the first expedition; and tarry only at the first Jew who stepped on the newly-discovered continent in a political mission, as it were: it was a Luis de Torres, a Jew, who had held a position with the Governor of Murcia, and who accepted baptism shortly before Columbus set sail.[1] As he knew Hebrew, Chaldee, and a little Arabic, Columbus employed him as interpreter with the Grand-Chan.

From Guanahani the admiral directed his course in a south-westerly direction and reached Cuba by the end of October, which he took to be the island of Cipangu. He did not want to extend for the present the expedition further toward the North and determined to send scouts into the interior of the country; he selected as one Luis de Torres, with Rodrigo de Jerez, of Ayamonte as companion. In the relation which Columbus rendered in Spanish to Luis de Santangel, the Beaconsfield of that time, and to Gabriel Sanchez, his brother-in-law, the treasurer of the Aragonian crown, as the financial patrons of his enterprise, it is stated: "I sent two men into the land to find out whether there was a king there, or large cities."[2] He furnished them with instructions, informed them what to say to the ruler in the name of the royal princes of Spain and how to prepare him for the conclusion of a treaty with the Castilian crown; he even handed them an autographic letter and presents.

On the 2nd of November Luis de Torres proceeded on his journey with his associate and returned to Columbus on the 6th of that month. He related how he had found after he had traveled about twelve miles, a place with fifty

---

[1] Herrera, Historia General, Dec. 1. L. 23.
[2] . . . enbie dos hombres por la tierra para saber si aina rey o grandes ciudades.

cabins and a population of about one thousand souls. The ruler of the country received the emissaries in a friendly manner and accompanied them with his son and one of his people to the admiral.[1]

Luis de Torres gained the friendship of the prince or cacique and settled in Cuba, where he received as a present not only extensive lands but also a number of slaves, five grown people and a child.[2]

---

[1] Franc. Ad. de Varnhagen, la verdadera Guanahani (Santiago, 1684), P. 31 ff.

[2] Documentos ineditos del Archivo de Indias, T. 1 P. 87 f.

The Rabbi Dr. Joseph Krauskopf, in a Sunday lecture, October 23, 1892, before the Reform Congregation Keneseth Israel, of Philadelphia, took for his theme "The Debt of the Oldest People to the Newest World," and devoted special attention to the part played by the Jews in Geographical exploration. Speaking of the expedition in 1492, Dr. Krauskopf said: "The Jews at that time, and long before, were noted as experienced travelers and venturesome explorers. Being driven from land to land, and obliged to speak, beside their own, the language of the people among whom they resided, being, besides, deeply interested in commerce, and carrying on an extensive trade with their brethren scattered all over the known world, they possessed an extraordinary knowledge of lands and peoples, and languages, and were especially fitted for purposes of exploration. Together with the Moors in Spain, they had become the most renowned astronomers and cosmographers of the world. Three hundred years before Columbus entered upon the scenes, the Spanish Rabbi Benjamin of Tudela, had penetrated into China and explored the islands of Southern Asia. Three centuries before Columbus dreamed of a shorter journey to India along the unknown western sea, Jewish and Moorish savans taught that the earth was a sphere, determined approximately its circumference and diameter, and declared that a journey westward over the sea of darkness must lead to the eastern shore of Asia. And before Columbus could venture out upon a wholly unknown sea, the learned cosmographer Martin Behaim of Nuremberg, had to call in the assistance of the Jewish mathematicians Moses, Rabbi Abraham, and the physician Vecinho, to construct a globe, and to perfect the astrolabe, to lessen therewith the dangers of navigation by enabling the sailors to measure by the altitude of the sun their distance from the equator and from the coast. The fondness for exploration has continued a characteristic of the Jew to this day. Jews accompanied Alexander von Humboldt and Agassiz. The explorers of Turkestan, Afghanistan, Abyssinia, were Jews. Greely's ill-fated North Pole expedition counted among its number the Jew Edward Israel, of Kalamazoo. Emil Bessel, a German Jew, was one of the members of Captain Hall's North Pole Expedition, and Kepes, a Hungarian Jew, accompanied Payers to the North Pole. Emin Pasha, the African explorer, is of the Hebrew race, as is also Vita Hassan, one of his brave rescuers; as is also our own Professor Angelo Heilprin, the leader of the Peary Relief Expedition. There is, therefore, nothing strange to find Jews accompanying Columbus on his journey over an unknown sea, nor is it improbable that they joined him of their own free will, either from love of adventure, or in the interest of knowledge, or in the interest of commerce." (Sunday Lectures of Joseph Krauskopf, Vol. VI., No. 1.)

IV.

CHRISTOPHER COLUMBUS IN ORIENTAL LITERATURE.[1]

Christopher Columbus in Oriental Literature, a subject of interest equally to students of oriental literature and of American history, has been investigated by M. Henry Harrisse to whom modern scholars are primarily indebted for the scientific investigation of all subjects having reference to Columbus and the early voyagers to America. Harrisse's brief yet comprehensive article on this subject (*Christoph Columbus im Orient*) appeared in the *Centralblatt für Bibliothekwesen*, Vol. X (1888), pp. 133–138. After enumerating the references to Columbus in Hebrew literature, Mr. Harrisse cites a Turkish work specially devoted to an account of the New World. This work was known as *Hadisi Nev* containing, however, as well an Arabic title *Tarih el Hind Gharby*, and was printed at Constantinople by Ibrahim Effendi (the renegade). The printing was completed April 3, 1730, and the book is therefore one of the incunabula of the Ottoman

---

[1] The above is an abstract of a communication made to the American Oriental Society by Dr. Cyrus Adler, of the Johns Hopkins University. In 1891, while visiting Constantinople as a special commissioner in the interest of the World's Columbian Exposition, Dr. Adler secured a rare manuscript of an early Turkish work, with maps and illustrations, relating to the New World and to Columbus. Dr. Adler hopes to publish a more complete description of this work.

press. Mr. Harrisse had access to the copy of this very rare work in the Library of the *École des langues orientales vivantes* in Paris. He was of opinion that the book was composed by Hadji Khalfa.

The article of Mr. Harrisse called forth some notes by Professor J. Gildemeister of Bonn, in the same volume of the same journal (pp. 303–306). Professor Gildemeister pointed out that if the book, *Hadisi Nev*, was written as stated by Mr. Harrisse, and in the Catalogue of the Library of von Hammer, under the reign of Murad III, 1574–95, it could not have been written by Hadji Halfa who was not born earlier than 1600.

No MS. of this work was known to either of these writers, nor apparently to von Hammer. While in Constantinople in 1891, I secured a well-written and well-preserved MS. of this work. It is dated in the year 77. On folio 38b the author alludes to the Turkish Admiral Khair-ed-din, surnamed Barbarossa, as having "recently died." His death took place in the year 956 of the Hegira so that 9 is apparently the number to be prefixed to 77, and the date would accordingly be 977, *i. e.* 1569–70. The MS. contains 13 colored illustrations of animals and plants of America, some of them executed with considerable fidelity. It also contains two diagrams and three colored maps. That of the new world represents South America with fair accuracy, and is in the opinion of Mr. Harrisse, in some respects unique. The maps in the MS. are of course much older than those in the printed work. An inferior MS. of the same work exists in the Library of the American Oriental Society, being very appropriately MS. No. 1 of the Society's collections. It was presented by Mr. J. P. Brown, Secretary and Dragoman of the United States Legation at Constantinople. Mr. Brown stated at the time (*Jr. Am. Or. Soc.*, Vol. I. p. xxix) that "It was quite the first work ever printed at Constantinople by the Turks. I cannot learn the name of the author. . . . I am informed that the Târîkh Hind Gharby existed in manuscript many years before the introduction of printing, but was taken up and printed on account of its popularity as a curious and amusing work." A copy of the printed work is now deposited in the Smithsonian Institution, being in the collection of the late Wm. B. Hodgson, which has been deposited in the Institution by the Telfair Academy of Arts and Sciences at Savannah, Ga. I hope shortly to publish the maps and illustrations in my MS. as well as a translation of those portions relating to Columbus.

APPENDIX.

I.

BIBLIOGRAPHIES OF THE DISCOVERY OF AMERICA.

By CHARLES WEATHERS BUMP, A. B.

It has not been attempted to make this list of bibliographies exhaustive and complete, although it will be found to contain more collective titles than any reference list or catalogue on the subject that has yet appeared. The plan of the compiler has been to exclude: 1st, public library catalogues and auction lists of Americana, because in them all references to the navigators included here may easily be found under their appropriate headings; 2d, earlier catalogues of first editions and *incunabula*, because they have been superseded by later and more exhaustive works, which are mentioned; 3d, books whose paucity of references makes them of but little use. With these exceptions an effort has been made to include the best lists of books on Columbus, Vespucius, John and Sebastian Cabot, and the more or less legendary navigators before the fifteenth century. Some titles may have been inadvertently omitted, and for any mention of such additional lists, the compiler will be grateful.

There is naturally more or less duplication of entries in the special bibliographies here enumerated, and a brief mention of those that are more or less complete, may not be out of place. Mr. Winsor's "History of America" contains in the critical chapters of the first three volumes, the latest and most exhaustive bibliographies on all of the subjects mentioned in this list. There are other works, however, to which attention may specially be called. In pre-Columbian literature, Mr. Watson's last edition will be found almost as extensive as Mr. Winsor's bibliography, and possibly better arranged; in rare editions of Columbus, no better guides can be found than Harrisse, Bartlett, or Major. The Boston Public Library *Bulletin* for October, 1892, contains the best list of modern books on Columbus. Harrisse has also compiled a bibliography of Columbus, which when it appears, will probably be complete and satisfactory. For the Cabots, Harrisse's bibliographical notes will again be found to be the best arranged and most valuable.

1. Pre-Columbian Claims.

ALLEN, FRANCIS A. "Polynesian antiquities a link between the ancient civilizations of Asia and America." 1883.

Gives references on the early connection of America and Asia by way of Polynesia. Printed in the Compte Rendu (p. 246) of the Congrès des Américanistes at Copenhagen.

AMERICAN BIBLIOPOLIST. New York, February, 1869, pp. 47–50.

"An excellent bibliography of the Madoc claim."

BANCROFT, HUBERT HOWE. "Native Races of America." Vol. V. (*Works*, v. 5). San Francisco, 1886. Chapter I., "On the Origin of the Americans," pp. 1–132.

Mr. Bancroft in this chapter, as indeed in all the chapters of his numerous volumes, is exhaustive in his references, so that in the foot-notes may be found a nearly complete bibliography of the autochthonous origin of the native races, the Atlantis myth, and more particularly the pre-Columbian voyages.

BANCROFT, HUBERT HOWE. "History of Central America." Vol. I. (*Works*, v. 6). San Francisco, 1886. Chapter I, pp. 67–90.

A general summary, with copious references, of the myths and discoveries before Columbus. It duplicates most of the titles quoted in Mr. Bancroft's volume on "Native Races," (*vide supra*), but valuable in itself for references to maps and atlases, and for a bibliographical account of the general literature on the subject.

BOSTON PUBLIC LIBRARY. "Bulletins." Vol. II, 1871–5, Nos. 30 and 34; Vol. III, 1875–8, No. 37.

A series of brief, critical and bibliographical notes on the discovery of America, appended in most cases to the entry of the title of some book on the subject recently received. The separate topics are as follows: No. 30, July, 1874, p. 257, " Northmen in America;" No. 34, July, 1875, p. 368, "Fusang, or, the Chinese discovery of America;" No. 37, April, 1876, pp. 65–69, "America before Columbus." The last is exceedingly valuable for its numerous references and notes; in addition to the pre-Columbian voyages, the literature of the Mexican and Peruvian civilizations is also treated. Nearly all the titles given were afterward used in Winsor's "History of America."

BOSTON PUBLIC LIBRARY. " A Chronological Index to Historical Fiction, including Prose Fiction, Plays and Poems." Third and enlarged edition. Part I. (*Bulletin*, No. 87, January, 1892), p. 298.

Gives titles of several plays and poems including Southey's "Madoc" and Longfellow's "Skeleton in Armor."

BOUCHER DE LA RICHARDERIE, GILLES. " Bibliothéque universelle des voyages." Paris, 1808. Vol. I., pp. 43–51.

Gives a partial bibliography of the discoveries of the Northman, with a brief account of the discovery of Vinland.

BRYANT, W. C. AND GAY, S. H. " Popular History of the United States." New York, 1876. Vol. I., chapter 3, "The Northmen in America," pp. 35–63, chapter 4, " Pre-Columbian Voyages Westward," pp. 64–91.

Contains foot-notes giving references to the more important and more popular works.

BROWN, MARIE A. " The Icelandic Discoverers of America." London, 1887.

Bibliography, pp. 209–13.

BURDER, G. " The Welsh Indians." London, 1797.

Copious references on the Welsh story, with many proofs not to be found elsewhere.

ELLIOTT, CHARLES W. " The New England History." Vol. I., pp. 36–7. Boston, 1857.

A brief summary of authorities on the Northmen in New England.

FISKE, JOHN. " The Discovery of America." Vol. I., chapter 2, " Pre-Columbian Voyages:" foot-notes to pp. 148–151, 154–7, 226, 253.

Appendix.

For his authorities on this chapter, Mr. Fiske acknowledges himself indebted to Mr. Winsor's "History of America," and to Mr. Watson's bibliography.

FOSTER, W. E. " Old South Lectures on American History, 1891. Reference for pararellel readings." Boston, 1891. 6 Broadsheets.

The first of these sheets is on "Pre-Columbian Voyages to America," and will be found an excellent guide to a short and popular course of reading on the subject.

GRAVIER, GABRIEL. " Découverte de L'Amérique par les Normands au Xe Siécle." Paris and Rouen, 1874.

The foot-notes are very rich in references to the voyages of the Northmen. A chapter is also included on the voyages of Madoc and Zeno.

HAVEN, SAMUEL F. "Archaeology of the United States" (Smithsonian Institution, *Contributions.* Vol. VIII, 1856). Chapter I, pp. 8–16. " Ante-Columbian Voyages, Theories and Speculations."

A brief general account, with foot-notes, of the stories of the discovery of America. References not very extended.

HUMBOLDT, ALEXANDER VON. " Examen critique de l'histoire de la géographie du nouveau continent." 3 vols. Paris, 1836–8.

Humboldt discusses in detail the stories of the discovery of America before the time of Columbus. The references will still be found useful. The German translation by Ideler possesses an index.

KOHL, J. G. " History of the Discovery of Maine " (*Maine Hist. Soc. Publications*, 2d Series, Vol. I). Portland, 1869.

Abundant references are found in chapter 2 on "The Discoveries of the Northmen," and in the first part of chapter 3 on "English Trading Expeditions in the 14th and 15th Centuries."

LELAND, CHARLES G. "Fusang, or the Discovery of America by Chinese Buddhist Priests in the Fifth Century." London, 1875.

The thirteenth chapter contains a review of the discussion between the advocates and opponents of the Chinese discovery of America; and in the fourteenth chapter may be found, in an article reprinted from the "Chinese Recorder and Missionary Journal," the titles of the greater part of the literature on the subject.

MICHAUD, LOUIS GABRIEL. " Nouvelle Biographie Universelle." Paris, 1858. Vol. 16, pp. 250–1; Art. " Eric."

Paragraph at the end mentions a few of the leading supporters of the Norse story.

NOTES AND QUERIES. 1st Ser., Vol. 1, p. 342, Vol. 2, pp. 109, 277, " America known to the Ancients." 2d Ser., Vol. 5, pp. 314, 386, 387, 458, " America discovered in the Eleventh Century."

The first series of notes is valuable for references to classical literature on the subject of a new world. The second is a brief review of the Norse question.

OLD SOUTH LEAFLETS. Published by the Directors of the Old South Studies in History. Boston. No. 31, " The Voyages to Vinland."

A brief popular bibliography of the subject, pp. 15–16.

PARKMAN, FRANCIS. " Pioneers of France in the New World." Boston, 1865, pp. 169–170.

Refers to the supporters of the historic claim of Cousin of Dieppe as a discoverer.

SLAFTER, REV. EDMUND F. " Voyages of the Northmen to America." Boston, printed for the Prince Society, 1877. Bibliographical Notes, pp. 127–42.

Mentions the principal works on the Norse voyages, with valuable descriptive and critical notes. The best bibliography in its special field, and particularly good when treating of the literature growing out of the publication of Professor Rafn's " Antiquitates Americanae."

VINING, E. P. " An inglorious Columbus; or, Evidence that Hwui Shăn and a party of Buddhist monks from Afghanistan discovered America in the fifth century, A. D." New York, 1885.

List of authorities and references will be found on pp. 711–40. "A repository of all the essential contributions to the question from De Guignes down."

WATSON, PAUL BARRON. " Bibliography of the Pre-Columbian Discoveries of America." (Library Journal, Vol. VI., No. 8, August, 1881, pp. 227–44. Reprinted in the third edition of R. B. Anderson's " America not discovered by Columbus," (Chicago, 1883), and also issued separately, (Boston, 1881).

" The present essay is intended as a complete bibliography of those claims to the discovery of America before Columbus, which are based upon documentary evidence." The best bibliography of the whole field of discovery before the time of Columbus. It is exceedingly well arranged and classified under its separate sub-divisions. The critical notes also form a valuable guide to the use of the materials indicated.

WINSOR, JUSTIN. "Narrative and Critical History of America." Boston, 1889. Vol. I., pp. 76–116, "Pre-Columbian Explorations."

One of the most valuable features of this connected series of historical monographs edited by Mr. Winsor, is the critical examination of sources at the end of each chapter. The critical essay in the chapter on "Pre-Columbian Explorations" is by Mr. Winsor himself, and is the most complete bibliography of the whole subject yet published. It is, however, open to an objection on the ground of its arrangement, which does not permit of easy reference. The essay on maps (pp. 117–132) will be found very useful.

2. COLUMBUS.

ATHENAEUM. August 31, 1889, p. 288. "Columbus' letter to Luis de Sant Angel."

Enumerates the reproductions and translations of this letter, in a brief review of Ellis and Elvey's edition of it.

AVEZAC, M. A. P. D'. "Année veritable de la Naissance de Christophe Colomb, etc." Paris, 1873 (also in *Societe de Geographie, Bulletin*, 6e series, t. 4, 1872).

Gives lists of authorities on the subject discussed.

BANCROFT, HUBERT HOWE. "History of Central America." Vol. I. (*Works*, v. 6). San Francisco, 1886.

The fourth chapter contains a careful study of the visits of "Columbus to the Coasts of Honduras, Nicaraugua, and Costa Rica," and in addition to numerous foot-notes, Mr. Bancroft gives (pp. 238–46) a good bibliography of Columbus, with a critical discussion of Irving and Prescott. Titles to books on Columbus may also be found at the bottom of pages 90–98, 109–11, and 119–20.

BARTLETT, JOHN R. "Bibliotheca Americana: A Catalogue of Books relating to North and South America in the library of John Carter Brown, of Providence." Second edition. 1875. Vol. I, covering the years 1482–1601.

"The most extensive printed list of all Americana previous to 1800, more especially anterior to 1700, which now exists. Numerous fac-similes of titles and maps add much to its value."— *Winsor*. Six hundred books are entered in this volume, which together with the catalogues of Harrisse, Major and Sabin (*vide infra*) leave but little to be desired by those who are making a study of the early editions of the writings of Columbus. There are older bibliographical works on Americana, notably those of Rich, Stevens, and Ternaux-Compans, but they have not been included in this list, because of later and more accessible works.

Bibliographies of the Discovery of America. 61

BOSTON PUBLIC LIBRARY. "Bulletins." Vol. II, 1871–5, No. 33; Vol. IV, 1879–81, No. 51.

Bulletin No. 51, October, 1879, p. 124, contains a brief bibliography of the controversy respecting the remains of Columbus. No. 33, April, 1875, pp. 340-1, will be found to contain lists of biographies, of the Great Admiral, of his writings, and of general narratives of his voyages. The critical notes are brief and useful.

BOSTON PUBLIC LIBRARY. " Catalogue of the Spanish Library . . . . bequeathed by George Ticknor. . . . (Compiled) by Jesse Lyman Whitney." Boston, 1879, pp. 92–5, Art. " Christopher Columbus," with Notes by Mr. Winsor.

Exceedingly useful summary in small compass of all the more valuable publications on Columbus, though necessarily a duplication to a great extent, of the notes previously published in the "Bulletin." Among the sub-divisions of the subject are biographies, voyages, maps, and portraits. This bibliography was reprinted in a separate pamphlet, in an edition of 30 copies, (Boston, 1876).

BOSTON PUBLIC LIBRARY. "A Chronological Index to Historical Fiction. Third and Enlarged Edition." (*Bulletin* No. 87, January, 1802, pp. 298–9.

Thirty-seven titles of plays, novels and poems on Columbus are given, and this will be still further enlarged in a final revision before the Index is issued separately.

BOSTON PUBLIC LIBRARY. Bulletin No. 90, October, 1892, pp. 221–33. "Columbus: a list of the writings of Christopher Columbus, and of the works relating to him, etc."

The most recent, the largest, and the best classified bibliography of Columbus that has yet been published. The subdivisions of the catalogue include letters of Columbus, his voyages, modern works about him, his portraits, birthplace and family, remains, and final place of burial, signature, and poems and novels about him.

BROCKEN, BARON VAN. " Des Vicissitudes Posthumes de Christophe Colomb, et de sa Béatification Possible." Leipsic and Paris, 1865.

Enumerates most of the publications bearing on the grounds for the canonization of Columbus.

BRUNET, JACQUES CHARLES. " Manuel du Libraire et de L'Amateur de Livres." Vol. II., Paris 1861, pp. 163–5.

Contains titles and descriptions of rarer and more important editions of the letters of Columbus.

BUDINGER, MAX. "Zur Columbus Literatur." Vienna, 1889.
Prof. Büdinger is one of the principal writers in the field of discussion opened by Harrisse, concerning the authenticity of Ferd. Columbus' life of his father. The references to the literature brought out by the subject are very full. The article is from the Mitt. der K. K. Geog. Gesell., 1889. (Vienna Acad. of Sciences.)

BUET, CHARLES. "Christophe Colomb." Paris, 1886, pp. 303–5.
Buet's authorities are mainly those writers who have followed the Catholic or idealistic treatment of the life of Columbus.

CANCELLIERI, FRANCESCO. "Notizie Storiche e Bibliografiche di Christoforo Colombo di Cuccaro nel Monferrato, Discopritore dell'America." Pp. 282, and index. Bound up with a similar work on Giovanni Gersen, abbot of S. Stefano in Vercelli, under the general title of "Dissertazionii Epistolar Bibliografiche Sopra Christoforo Colombo, etc." Rome, 1809.
Exceedingly valuable, particularly for its references to the extensive Columbus literature written on the continent before the nineteenth century, of which but few titles can be found in American libraries. The ninety-two chapters or sections of the book (the number possibly selected with design), contain discussions of every topic in the life of Columbus, all of them written in the style and with the vast amount of unimportant detail usually displayed by eighteenth century historians. The author favors, as may be noticed from the title, the view that Columbus was born at Cuccaro.

CENTRALBLATT FÜR BIBLIOTHEKSWESEN. Vol. IX., No. 3, March, 1892, pp. 105–122. "Qui a imprimé la premiére lettre de Colomb."
An excellent discussion, with abundant notes and references, of the question of the first edition.

CENTRALBLATT FÜR BIBLIOTHEKSWESEN. "Christoph Colombus im Orient," by Henry Harrisse. Vol. X, 1888, pp. 133–8. Also article on the same subject, by Prof. J. Gildermeister, of Bonn, on pp. 303–6 of the same volume.
A translation of these brief but comprehensive articles has been made by Dr. Cyrus Adler, and will shortly be published in the proceedings of the American Oriental Society. An abstract appears in this number of the *Studies*.

ENCYCLOPAEDIA BRITANNICA. Ninth edition. Vol. VI. Article "Columbus," p. 176 English edition, p. 158 American edition.
In the bibliographical appendix to the article, twenty-seven of the more important biographies of Columbus are enumerated.

FISKE, JOHN. "The Discovery of America." 2 vols. Boston, 1892. Vol. I., chapter 5, pp. 335–342.

A sketch of the various conflicting views of the principal biographers of Columbus.

FOX, CAPT. G. V. "An Attempt to solve the Problems of the first Landing Place of Columbus in the New World." Appendix No. 18 to the Report of the Superintendent of the U. S. Coast and Geodetic Survey for 1880. (Senate Documents, 3d session, 46th Congress, pp. 349–52.)

Gives a list of the writers supporting the claims of each of the islands supposed to have been the landing place of Columbus in 1492. Capt. Fox's accurate researches have done much toward modifying the views of those whom he mentions on these pages.

GRAESSE, J. T. G. "Trésor de Livres Rares et Precieux." Dresden, 1861. Vol. II., pp. 228–9. "Supplement," Dresden, 1869, p. 196.

Titles, notes, and descriptions of a few of the editions and translations of the writings of Columbus.

HARRISSE, HENRY. "Bibliotheca Americana Vetustissima. A Description of Works relating to America published between the years 1492 and 1551." New York, 1866, pp. liv, 519.
—— "Additions," Paris, 1872, pp. xl, 199.

Indispensable for descriptions of all the early editions of the writings of Columbus, or of early accounts of his discoveries. Foot-notes and a careful index include several hundred additional references to later works. The chronological appendix at the end of the supplementary volume will also be found useful.

HARRISSE, HENRY. "Notes on Columbus." New York. Privately printed in 1866, pp. vii, 227.

"Ninety copies only printed for presentation, at the expense of Samuel L. M. Barlow, of New York. . . . It is both bibliographical and historical, and in each department is a specimen of zeal and erudition."—*Sabin.*
The small number of copies printed has made the book quite rare, and it can only be found in a few of the leading public libraries of America. It is the first fruit of Mr. Harrisse's life-long studies on the great Genoese (*vide infra*).

HARRISSE, HENRY. "Christophe Colomb, son origine, sa vie, ses voyages, sa famille, et ses descendants." Paris. 2 vols. 1884.

"If any one," says Mr. Winsor, "desires to compass all the elucidations and guides which a thorough student of the career and fame of Columbus would wish to consider, the foot-notes in Harrisse's *Christophe Colomb* would probably, most essentially, shorten his labors. Harrisse, who has prepared, but not yet published, lists of the books devoted to Columbus *exclusively*, says that they number about six hundred titles." Mr. Harrisse has devoted the major part of the last thirty years to a study, from new and original sources, of Christopher and Ferdinand Columbus, and the results of his work are to be seen in a score of volumes in various European languages. A complete list of his works, forming in itself a valuable Columbus bibliography, may be found at the close of his latest work on "The Discovery of North America." (London and Paris, 1892.)

HESSELS, J. H. "Essai sur les éditions de la première lettre de Colomb imprimées avant 1500." (*Bibliophile Belge.*, 6e année, pp. 93–121, 1871.

This article, the title of which explains itself, has been translated into English, through the coöperation of Mr. Major, who made use of the same sources as Mr. Hessels in preparing his bibliography.

HISTORICAL MAGAZINE. Vol. V, No. 2, February, 1861, pp. 33–38. "A Bibliographical Account of the Voyages of Columbus."

Reprinted from Mr. James Lenox's privately printed work on the second voyage of Columbus, "Nicolaus Syllacius de Insulis Nuper Inventis." Fifteen editions of the four voyages are carefully described. Mr. Lenox's book contains many cuts and reproductions omitted in this reprint.

HISTORISCHE ZEITSCHRIFT, 1887; whole number, Vol. LVII, new series, Vol. XXI, pp. 222–234. "Die Neuere Columbus-Literatur," von Konrad Haebler.

A discriminative review of thirty-one books on Columbus, mainly on those produced by the triangular discussion between Harrisse, D'Avezac and Peragallo, respecting the authenticity of Ferdinand's biography of his father. The new theories recently presented on subjects connected with Columbus are all touched upon, and their literature indicated.

HUMBOLDT, ALEXANDER VON. "Examen critique de l'histoire de la géographie du Nouveau continent." 3 vols. Paris, 1836–8.

Humboldt was one of the first to approach Columbus from the standpoint of documentary history. His references will be found useful.

JAHRESBERICHTE DER GESCHICHTSWISSENSCHAFT. Berlin, 1887–92.

This excellent periodical of current historical literature is particularly full of references on Columbus in the years quoted. The earlier numbers of the annual also contain a few brief reviews of Columbus literature.

LAROUSSE, PIERRE. "Grand dictionnaire universel du XIXe Siécle." Paris, 1869. Vol. IV., pp. 635-7.

Appendix to article on Columbus contains descriptions and critical reviews of the leading poems and dramas on the great Genoese, with a brief mention of similar paintings and statues.

LITERARY NEWS. Vol. XIII., No. 10, October, 1892, pp. 309-10. "New books about Columbus."

Mentions and briefly describes the literature brought out by the centennial of the discovery.

MAJOR, R. H. "Bibliography of the first Letter of Columbus," in his "Select Letters of Columbus," second edition. London, 1870. (Hakluyt Society.) Pp. cviii-cxlii. Also issued separately, London, 1872.

Deals only with the *incunabula* of the letter, and not with modern editions. The arrangement is strictly chronological.

MICHAUD, LOUIS GABRIEL. "Nouvelle Biographie Universelle." Paris, 1854, Vol. 8, pp. 636-7. Art. "Christophe Colomb."

The writings of Columbus are described and their most accessible editions indicated. The more important of the continental writers on the "Great Admiral" are also enumerated.

OLD SOUTH LEAFLETS. Published by the Directors of the Old South Studies in History. Boston.

Each number consists of a reprint of some important historical document or narrative, with a brief popular bibliography appended. Those connected with Columbus thus far published are : No. 29, "The Discovery of America;" No. 32, "Marco Polo's Account of Japan and Java;" No. 33, "Columbus' Letter to Gabriel Sanchez."

ROSELLY DE LORGUES, COMTE. "Christophe Colomb. Histoire de sa vie et de ses voyages." Paris, 1864. 2 vols.

The author is the most prominent of those writers who seek to subvert history and prove the religious purity of Columbus' life in order to secure canonization for him. In his introduction to this volume a review of the previous authorities on Columbus is undertaken and continued in his later works, "L'Ambassadeur de Dieu" (pp. 46-55), and "L'Histoire Posthume de Colombo," though in a very controversial manner. (Barry's translation of "Christophe Colomb," omits a number of the authorities noted by de Lorgues.) A better account of the literature on "St. Christopher" may be found in Baron van Brocken (*q. v.*).

RUELENS, C. "La première relation de Christophe Colomb, 1493." Lettre sur une édition de l' "Epistola Christofori Colom, appartenant à la Bibliothèque royale de Bruxelles." Brussels, 1885. Fac-similes.

I have not seen this work, of which the title seems sufficiently explanatory. A copy of it is in the Boston Public Library.

SABIN, JOSEPH. "A Dictionary of Books relating to America from the Discovery to the present time." New York, 1871. Vol. IV., pp. 274-285.

Fifty titles, including the earliest editions of the writings of Columbus, and of the rarer books concerning him, are mentioned. Mr. Sabin has borrowed nearly all the titles from Harrisse and Major. It is scarcely necessary to mention that in this work, under the names of early writers on America and Columbus, may be found most valuable notes and information on editions, on the history of the rarer volumes, and on their contents.

URICOECHEA, E. "Mapoteca Colombiana. Coleccion de los titulos de todos los mapas, planos, vistas, etc., relativos a la América Espãnola, Brasil, é isles adyacentes. Arreglada cronologicamente i precedida de una introduccion sobre la historia cartográfica de América." London, 1860.

One of the best accounts of early American cartography.

WINSOR, JUSTIN. "Christopher Columbus and How he received and imparted the Spirit of Discovery." Boston, 1891.

Chapter 1, pp. 1-30 is exceedingly valuable for a connected sketch of "Sources, and the Gatherers of them." Chapter 2, pp. 31-70, "Biographers and Portraits" contains an excellent summary of the two subjects.

WINSOR, JUSTIN. "Narrative and Critical History of America." Boston, 1889. Vol. II., pp. 24-128, "Columbus and His Discoveries;" pp. 204-30, "Companions of Columbus."

The first essay is by Mr. Winsor, and is the most complete Columbus bibliography thus far published. Mr. Edward Channing contributes the second *critique*.

3. VESPUCCI AND THE CABOTS.

BANCROFT, HUBERT HOWE. "History of Central America." Vol I. (*Works*, v. 6). San Francisco, 1886.

Abundant references to Vespucci may be found in the notes at the bottom of pp. 99-107, 112-13, 118; to the Cabots, on pp. 107-9, 113.

BOSTON PUBLIC LIBRARY. "Bulletins," No. 38, July, 1876. Vol. II, pp. 103-106. "Early Explorations in America."

Valuable guide to the literature on the voyages of the Cabots and Vespucci.

FOSTER, W. E. "Monthly Reference Lists." Vol. IV, No. 8, August, 1884, pp. 27–9. "Early English Explorations of America."
An excellent list for popular reading on the voyages of the Cabots and their English successors.

HARRISSE, HENRY. " Jean et Sebastien Cabot, Leur Origine et Leurs Voyages." Bibliographie, pp. 367–75. Paris, 1882.
The best bibliography yet prepared on the Cabots. Contains fifty-eight references, carefully arranged. Harrisse says in his preface: " Nous n'avons inséré dans cette bibliographie que les ouvrages: 1º, concernant les Cabots écrits par leur contemporains; 2º, consacrés exclusivement à ces navigateurs; 3º, contenant des assertions ou des indications qui ne se trouvent pas ailleurs."

KOHL, J. G. " History of the Discovery of Maine." (*Maine Hist. Soc. Publications*, 2d series, Vol. I.) Portland, 1869.
Chapter IV treats of the Cabots, and is supplied with abundant references and foot-notes.

NEW ENGLAND HISTORICAL AND GENEALOGICAL REGISTER. Vol. XV, 1861, April, July, pp. 97–104, 205–16. " A Bibliographical Essay on the Early Collections of Voyages to America," by Hon. William Willis.
A chronological sketch which should save much trouble to those who are looking for accounts of Columbus, Vespucci and the Cabots, in the old, and, in many cases, rare collections of early voyages. The contents of Hakluyt, De Bry, De Laet, Herrera, Navarrete, and other compilations are briefly analyzed.

OLD SOUTH LEAFLETS. Published by the Directors of the Old South Studies in History. Boston. No. 34, " Amerigo Vespucci's Account of his First Voyage; " No. 37, " The Voyages of the Cabots."
Brief, popular, reference lists will be found at the end of each number.

SANTAREM, M. LE VICOMTE DE. " Recherches Historiques, Critiques, et Bibliographiques sur Améric Vespuce et ses voyages." Paris, 1842.
The author is quite voluminous in his citations and criticisms of books or paragraphs bearing on Vespucius, and an excellent index makes it of easy reference.

STEPHEN, LESLIE. " Dictionary of National Biography." London, 1888. Vol. VIII., p. 171; Art. " Cabot."
An excellent bibliography in small compass.

VARNHAGEN,.F. A. DE. "Amerígo Vespucci, son Caractère, ses
Écrits, (Même les moins authentiques) sa vie, et ses naviga-
tions." Lima, 1865.

—— " Le Premier voyage de Amerigo Vespucci." Vienna, 1869.

—— " Nouvelles Recherches sur les derniers voyages du naviga-
teur Florentin." Vienna, 1870.

A good authority on the bibliography of the naming of America, and on
the editions of Vespucci's letters, but not very well arranged for reference.
The last monograph is particularly useful to the bibliographer.

WINSOR, JUSTIN. Narrative and Critical History of America."
Boston, 1889. Vol. II, pp. 153–179, "Vespucius and the
Naming of America; Vol. III, pp. 7–58, "The Voyages of
the Cabots."

The chapter on Vespucci is by Mr. Winsor, and is the best reference list
on the subject. The bibliography of the Cabots, by Mr. Charles Deane,
contains more titles than Mr. Harrisse's, but the latter is preferable on
account of its superior arrangement

II.

PUBLIC MEMORIALS TO COLUMBUS.[1]

By CHARLES WEATHERS BUMP, A. B.

1. INTRODUCTORY.

Nearly a century ago a well-known French geographer, M. de Fleurieu, expressed some indignation that "not an isle, not a cape, not a single place in the new world" honored itself and the great Admiral by sharing his name. The learned German, von Humboldt, and the scholarly Italian monk, Cancellieri, also have regretted that no monument, no statue, no memorial tablet to Columbus, showed the gratitude of the new world that owed its historic origin to him. Such statements are commonly accepted and believed in long after they have ceased to contain any truth whatever. Even now, nearly a century after their original utterance, we hear them repeated with all the fervor of absolute belief. Of national monuments to Columbus, it is true we have only a few, but local co-operation and private generosity have done so much that to-day it is probable that, with the single exception of Washington, no individual was ever honored to such a degree as the great Genoese. Sixty-five public memorials of him have either been erected or are nearly completed. Of these forty-two were in place before

---

[1] In compiling this catalogue of monuments and statues and other public memorials that have been raised in honor of the discoverer of America, I have used as my chief sources of information, notes from periodicals, from illustrated weeklies, the daily press, guide books, and books of travel. Frequent use has also been made of a manuscript on the subject kindly lent the writer by Mr. F. A. Ober, now of Washington, who is well qualified to speak upon the world's tributes to Columbus, from his long residence among Spanish speaking peoples. When the work was nearly completed, I received an advance copy of *The Chautauquan* for November, 1892, containing an illustrated article on the monuments to Columbus by Mr. William Eleroy Curtis. Had my own work been in a less advanced state, I should perhaps have abandoned the field to Mr. Curtis. As it is, I must acknowledge my indebtedness to him for the mention of four memorials which I had overlooked—the bust in Brooklyn, the Columbus statue in the Mexican Museum, the statue of Columbus at Colon in Cuba, and the proposed arch in Washington. A careful comparison of these two papers shows also that I have included fifteen memorials completed, or projected, which Mr. Curtis does not mention, and it is probable that there are others still, of which neither of us have heard.

the present Columbian year, and eight have been unveiled during that time. The United States alone contributes twenty-seven memorials to the great discoverer, and the islands of the West Indies, twelve. The Spanish government, by a liberal competition among native artists, has not only raised the standard of the fine arts, but has also contributed most beautiful and enduring national monuments to Columbus in Madrid, Havana, Barcelona, and Granada. In the United States individual generosity and the good will of Italian and Spanish residents have taken the place of public munificence, although a bill is at present in Congress to erect a suitable public memorial in Washington.

M. de Fleurieu's remark also seems sadly out of place when we attempt to enumerate the points on the earth's surface, whether created by Nature or man, that owe the origin of their name to the great Admiral. Mr. G. Brown Goode, of the Smithsonian Institution, has demonstrated this in a practical way on a map of the United States recently sent to the exposition at Madrid, in which each town, each river, each district bearing the name of Columbus or Columbia have been appropriately indicated.[1] In order to see the extent of the honors paid to Columbus we have but to reflect that nearly every state of this country possesses a town of his name; that among cities we have Columbus in Ohio, Georgia, Indiana and Mississippi, Colon in Panama and Cuba, Columbia in South Carolina and Pennsylvania; that among institutions of learning we have Columbia College and Columbian University; that the capital of the United States is situated in a District called Columbia; that one of the great rivers emptying into the Pacific has the same name; that one of the greatest states of South America bears a Spanish form of it; and that Great Britain, whose people were benefited most by the voyage of the great discoverer, has preserved the modified form of his name in one of their colonies in the world he discovered.

2. THE UNITED STATES.

1792. BALTIMORE. CHEVALIER D'ANMOUR'S MONUMENT.

On the grounds of the Samuel Ready Orphan Asylum in Baltimore, stands a tall shaft to Columbus, erected just one hundred years ago, on what was then his own estate, by Chevalier d'Anmour, who was the first French consul in Maryland. For nearly thirty years this was the only Columbus memorial in the New World, and for over fifty years the only one in the United States. It is an obelisk forty-four feet and four inches high, made of stuccoed brick. The base is about six and one-half feet square and the top about two and one half feet square. The base is about

---

[1] On Dr. Goode's map no less than one hundred and fifteen Columbian names have been found in our country alone, to say nothing of British Columbia or Columbian names in Central and South America. It is, however, an interesting fact that most of these names in the United States are east of the Mississippi river.

Public Memorials to Columbus. 71

two and one half feet high, with well-rounded corners of moulded brickwork. The pedestal proper is five and one half feet square, ten feet in height, and is surmounted by a capstone about one and one half feet high. From this point the obelisk narrows gradually toward the top. On the west side of the pedestal is a marble slab about two and one-half by four feet, upon which is the following inscription: "Sacred to the memory of Chris Columbus, Octob. XII, MDCCVIIIC." An account of the monument, with illustrations, appeared in *The Baltimore American* for August 4, 1891; in *Frank Leslie's Illustrated Weekly* for December 20, 1890; and in *The Baltimore Sun* for October 11 and 13, 1892; and in *The Chautauquan* for November, 1892. See also Dr. Adams' address on "Columbus," pp. 30–33.

1842. WASHINGTON. PAINTING IN THE CAPITOL ROTUNDA.

The familiar painting of the "Landing of Columbus," shown in one of the panels of the Capitol Rotunda, was completed in 1842, by John Vanderlyn, of New York, with whom a committee of Congress had contracted for the work in 1836, the selection of the subject being left to the choice of the artist. Mr. Vanderlyn had won considerable fame by previous pictures representing scenes in American history, but the present memorial of Columbus is not regarded as one of his best works. As one critic has remarked: "It feebly expresses what the artist set out to illustrate on canvas, and affords but little satisfaction to those who look at it." Mr. Vanderlyn received $10,000 from the government for his production, which has become so familiar to every American by frequent engravings and lithographs, and more especially by being engraved on the back of the $5 national bank note.

1846. WASHINGTON. PERSICO'S STATUE AT THE CAPITOL.

The second memorial in honor of Columbus from the National Government, is the semi-colossal group of statuary at the east front of the Capitol. The group is the work of Luigi Persico, an Italian, then resident in this country, and the sculptor of other pieces of statuary at the Capitol. It was done at his studio in Naples. Columbus is represented as holding the globe, on which is carved the name "America." A nude Indian girl, crouches, awe-stricken at his side. The figure of Columbus is encased in armor, said to be a correct copy "to the rivet" of the armor he wore. Persico was given the commission in 1837, and completed it in 1846. Twenty-eight thousand dollars was paid to him for the work, by successive acts of Congress.

1849. BOSTON. STATUE IN LOUISBURG SQUARE.

The first Boston statue to the great Discoverer was the one presented to the city in 1849, by Mr. Joseph Iasigi, a Grecian merchant, who afterward became an American citizen, and whose descendants are well known in Boston. The statue which was erected in Louisburg Square, is of marble, and represents Columbus in his youth. It was carved at Leghorn, and, as an artistic work, is entirely devoid of merit.

1864. WASHINGTON. THE COLUMBUS DOOR IN THE CAPITAL.

The massive bronze door at the Capitol, leading from the old House of Representatives to the new, was modelled by Randolph Rogers, the American sculptor, in 1858 at his studio in Rome, and cast at Munich in 1860, by F. Von Miller, although not put into position until 1864. It is nineteen feet in height and nine feet wide, weighs 20,000 pounds, and cost $28,000, of which $8,000 was received by Rogers for his share in the work. In the top of the arch stands a bust of Columbus, while on the doors are depicted scenes from the life of Columbus, eight on the square panels and one on the transom panel above. The incidents represented are: (1) The examination of Columbus at Salamanca; (2) Departure from La Rabida for the Spanish Court; (3) Before Ferdinand and Isabella; (4) Departure from Palos; (5) Landing at San Salvador; (6) First encounter with the Indians; (7) Triumphal entry into Barcelona; (8) Columbus in Chains; (9) His Death Bed. Around the door and between the panels are statues of prominent contemporaries of the navigators and busts of his historians. The doors were described in an illustrated article in *Harper's Weekly* for January 30, 1892.

1869. NEW YORK. STEBBINS STATUE AT CENTRAL PARK.

In the year 1869, the late Marshall O. Roberts presented to the city authorities of New York, a granite statue of Columbus for erection in Central Park. The gift was executed in Rome in 1867, by Miss Emma Stebbins, the friend and biographer of Charlotte Cushman, and the designer of the statue of Horace Mann in Boston, and the large Fountain at the Mall in Central Park. It is seven feet high, and represents Columbus in the garb of a sailor, with a mantle thrown over his shoulder, grasping a tiller with his right hand. The face is copied from "accepted portraits of the Giovian type." The statue has never been erected, and is now stored away in an old arsenal in the zoölogical garden.

1872. BOSTON. STATUE IN MUSEUM OF FINE ARTS.

In 1872, Mr. A. P. Chamberlaine, of Concord, Mass., presented to the city of Boston a marble statue by Giulio Monteverde, of Genoa, called "The First Inspirations of the Boy Columbus." The statue was executed at Rome in the preceding year, and received the first gold medal at Parma a few months afterward. It is one of the most beautiful sculptures illustrative of the great Admiral. He is seated upon the capstan of a vessel, with an open book in his hand, his foot carelessly swinging in an iron ring hanging from a staple in the capstan. The statue was at first placed in the Boston Athenæum, but, on the opening of the new Museum of Fine Arts in 1876, it was transferred to that building, and is now in the hall on the first floor devoted to works in marble. A representation of it appeared as a frontispiece to *The Chautauquan* for November, 1892.

1875. PHILADELPHIA. ITALIAN STATUE IN FAIRMOUNT PARK.

In 1875, the Italian citizens of Philadelphia defrayed the cost of the erection of a marble statue to the Genoese navigator, which was presented to the Centennial Commission in the succeeding year, and has since stood in Fairmount Park, opposite Horticultural Hall. It is of heroic size, a standing figure, the right hand resting on a globe, and the left holding a chart. An anchor and a rope are emblematic of the career of the great sailor. On the pedestal are bas-reliefs representing the landing of Columbus, and the coat of arms of the United States and Italy. An illustration of the statue appeared in the *Philadelphia Times* for October 9, 1892.

1883. SACRAMENTO, CAL. COLUMBUS AND ISABELLA.

In the centre of the rotunda of the State Capitol at Sacramento stands a group of three figures—Columbus, Queen Isabella, and a page—in which the great navigator is represented as explaining to Her Catholic Majesty his theory of a western route to the Indies. The statuary is the work of Meade, the sculptor, and was presented to the State by D. O. Mills, a former resident.

1886. ST. LOUIS. THE SHAW STATUE.

In 1886, Mr. Henry D. Shaw, one of St. Louis' best known citizens, presented the city with a gilt bronze statue of Columbus, of heroic size, modelled and cast by Müller at Munich. The statue was erected at the east end of Tower Grove Park, another of Mr. Shaw's generous gifts, on a high granite pedestal, upon the sides of which are four bronze panels representing prominent events in his career. The face of the statue is copied from that at Genoa and the great Admiral is represented as looking forward with an expression half anxious, half triumphant, to the light which he has seen to the westward, and which betokens the nearness of the land. The statue was unveiled on October 12, 1886, and an account of it may be found in *The Nation* for October 28, of that year.

1892. NEW YORK. ITALIAN MONUMENT.

The most important memorial to Columbus yet raised in the United States is the one which was presented to the City of New York by the

Italians of the New World, and unveiled with appropriate ceremonies, on October 12, 1892, in the southwest corner of Central Park. The monument was the work of Professor Gaetano Russo, of Rome, whose competitive design was selected by a committee of fifteen, appointed by the Italian government. From the square base, of Boveno granite, on which are bronze bas-reliefs representing the first sight of land and the actual landing, a circular column of granite, rises to the height of sixty-one feet. This, in turn, is surmounted by a statue of Columbus, in Carrara marble, fourteen feet high, making a total height of seventy-five feet. Towards the base of the granite column, on opposite sides, are two groups, the one in marble representing the Genius of Geography, the other a bronze eagle holding in its claws the shields of the United States and Genoa. Six *rostra*, also of bronze, project from opposite sides of the column. The cost of the memorial was $35,000. The money was collected from Italians resident in North America, with liberal aid also from the Italian government. The subscription was begun and carried through by Chevalier Barsotti, the proprietor of the Italian paper published in New York, *Progresso Italo-Americano*. It was brought to this country in an official transport of the Italian government, which also displayed its interest in the monument by ordering several men-of-war here for the dedication ceremonies. A description, with complete illustrations will be found in *Harper's Weekly*, Vol. XXXVI, p. 805; Cf. also in the *Review of Reviews* for October, 1892; *Frank Leslie's Illustrated Paper* for October 13, and the daily papers of New York for October 12 and 13.

1892. NEW YORK. COLUMBIAN ARCH.

During the Columbian festivities in New York in October, 1892, there stood at 58th Street and Fifth Avenue a temporary arch in honor of the discoverer of America. The arch was erected at a cost of $8,000, from the prize design of Henry B. Herts, a student of Columbia College. To replace the arch by a lasting memorial of the same design in white marble, for which the Columbian Committee are now soliciting subscriptions, will cost over $350,000. Mr. Herts' design was suggested by the Arch of Constantine at Rome. The total height of the structure will be 160 feet and its total width 120; the opening of the arch will be 80 feet high by 40 feet wide. On the front of each pier will be a large marble fountain, lighted at night by electricity, the water playing about figures of Victory and Immortality. Above each fountain will be a panel, one representing Columbus at the Court of Spain, the other at the Convent of La Rabida. Panels in the attic will contain white marble illustrations of the entry of Columbus in Madrid. The crowning figure of the arch will be an allegorical group representing Columbus discovering America, from the deck of a ship about to cast anchor off an unknown shore. To the right and left will be bronze groups, emblematical of North and South America welcoming the advent to their continent of the new life, which is represented by a cluster statue of Exploration, Science and Art. An illustration of Mr. Herts' design, with others not accepted, will be found in *Harper's Weekly*, September 17, 1892.

1892. BALTIMORE. ITALIAN STATUE IN DRUID HILL PARK.

On the 12th of October, 1892, there was unveiled, in Druid Hill Park, the second Baltimore monument to Columbus, presented by the Italian residents of the city, under the leadership of Mr. Vito Pipitone. The statue, which was designed by Achille Canessa in Genoa, is six feet and a half in height, and together with the pedestal rises about eighteen feet from the base. Columbus stands erect against the stone balustrade of a quay, from which depends a heavy ring, such as would be used for mooring a vessel. In his right hand he grasps a half-rolled chart, and his left hand rests easily upon a globe placed upon the balustrade. The inscription on the pedestal reads: "To Christoforo Colombo. The Italians of Baltimore, 1892." Illustrations of the monument have appeared in the *Baltimore Sun* of August 19, and October 13, 1892, in the *Baltimore American* for October 13, and the *Evening News* for October 12.

1892. BOSTON. THE BUYENS STATUE.

In September, 1892, the City Council of Boston decided to honor the fourth centennial year of the discovery of America, by the dedication of a duplicate of the statue which a Boston committee was then having cast for erection at Isabella, the first settlement in the New World (*q. v.*). Copley Square (where stand the new Public Library, the Museum of Fine Arts, Trinity Church, and other buildings of architectural beauty), was at first selected as a proper place for the Columbus statue, but upon an exhibition of the model, so much adverse criticism was passed upon it, that the State Art Commission refused to allow the work to be placed there. The dispute between the friends and opponents of the statue was finally closed by its erection and dedication, October 21, in front of the Catholic Cathedral of the Holy Cross. The statue was taken largely from designs drawn by Richard Andrew, a student at the State Normal Art School, Boston, the sculptor being Alois Buyens, of Ghent, the designer of an heroic statue of President Brand, of the Orange Free State. It is of colossal size, representing Columbus giving thanks to God. The left arm is outstretched, while his right hand points to the site of the first settlement at Isabella on a globe at his side. Bas-reliefs representing the genius of Christianity and the genius of civilization are on opposite sides of the pedestal.

1892. HARRISBURG, PENN. MONUMENT.

On October 21, "Columbus Day," at Harrisburg, Pa., there was unveiled, in the grounds of St. Patrick's Cathedral, a small monument to the immortal Genoese. The dedication was preceded by a parade and by appropriate exercises at the Cathedral.

1892. NEWARK, N. J. ITALIAN MEDALLION.

Columbus Day was celebrated at Newark, N. J., by the unveiling, in the City Hall, of a bronze relief medallion of Columbus presented by the united Italian societies of the city. The work was modelled by J. Moneta, of New York, and measures 3 ft. 2 in. by 2 ft. 7 in. The medallion of Columbus, whose portrait is given full-faced, is supported by the coats of arms of Italy and the United States, held by an eagle and a lion. On each side of the medallion is seated a female figure: America on the right holds aloft the torch of civilization, as she crowns the discoverer with the laurel wreath that frames the medallion; Italy, on the left, points to the date of the discovery on the scroll of history she holds. A description and illustration of the medallion appeared in the *N. Y. Herald* for October 21.

1892. WILLIMANTIC, CONN. STATUE OF COLUMBUS.

Willimantic, Connecticut, celebrated Columbus day by dedicating to him a statue, secured through popular subscriptions. The work was purchased in Belgium by thê Rev. Flerimóna de Bruycker, pastor of one of the Catholic churches of the town.

——. BROOKLYN, N. Y. HISTORICAL SOCIETY'S BUST.

The most conspicuous ornament on the building of the Long Island Historical Society in Brooklyn, is a terra-cotta bust of Columbus of modern but artistic workmanship, by Olin F. Warner of New York. Mr. Warner took for his model the bust at Genoa, but introduced some changes in costume.

——. NEW YORK. HISTORICAL SOCIETY'S BUST.

The New York Historical Sociėty possesses a duplicate of the ideal bust of Columbus in the Capitoline Museum at Rome. I have been unable to find any record of this accession by the Society.

——. WASHINGTON. BUST IN THE WHITE HOUSE.

In the main vestibule of the White House stands a bust in marble. Its origin and history are alike unknown.

(Projected.) CHICAGO. WORLD'S FAIR STATUE.

A statue of Columbus, modelled by Howard Kretschmar, and erected by the Directory of the Columbian Exposition at a cost of $40,000, will be unveiled next year. An illustration of the statue appeared in *Harper's Weekly* for April 25, 1891, and in the *N. Y. Herald* for October 22, 1892.

(Projected). COLUMBUS, OHIO. MONUMENT.

The people of Columbus, O., have decided to raise a suitable monument in this centennial year to the man for whom their city was named. The work has not yet been erected, although the statue has been modelled and cast. It is a single figure, of sheet copper, ten feet high, and represents Columbus as "a man of thought and mind, rather than as a man of action." The work on it was done entirely by citizens of Ohio, the sculptor being Alphons Pelzer, of Columbus, and the moulder, W. H. Mullins, of Salem. An illustration of the statue appeared in the plates of the *American Architect* for October 22 of this year.

(Projected). NEW YORK. SPANISH FOUNTAIN.

The Spanish residents of New York, not to be outdone by their Italian brethren, have offered to the city authorities, for erection in Central Park, a fountain in honor of Columbus. The sculptor is Mr. Fernando Miranda, a resident of New York, but a former pupil of Señor Piquer, who designed the Columbus statue at Cardenas. Mr. Miranda's plan is to have a stone basin of 100 feet diameter, from the centre of which rises a globe. With one foot on Florida and the other on the West Indies, stands Columbus with his sword grasped firmly in his right hand. On each side of him, and holding to him eagerly in their excitement, is one of the brothers Pinzon, the one pointing to some distant point, the other scanning the horizon. The total height of the globe and the figure of Columbus is 29 feet, the latter being 16 feet high. The material is to be bronze, and the donors have endeavored to procure contributions of bronze from every Spanish-speaking country in the world. A description and illustration of the fountain appeared in *Harper's Weekly* for June 11, 1892.

(Projected). WASHINGTON. NATIONAL MONUMENT.

On December 16, 1891, Senator Morrell introduced into the Senate a joint resolution for the erection of a monument to Columbus at the western entrance to the Capitol grounds, at the head of Pennsylvania Avenue. Seventy-five thousand dollars were set aside for this purpose by the resolution, which passed the Senate on April 15, 1892. In the House of Representatives it was referred to the Committee on the Library, and not reported before the recess. The measure will perhaps be taken up again at the coming session of Congress.

(Projected). WASHINGTON. TRIUMPHAL ARCH.

During the present year a movement was started among the citizens of Washington to erect a triumphal arch in honor of Columbus. The site proposed for the arch was on the high ground at the crest of the hill at the end of Sixteenth Street.

3. THE WEST INDIES.

1822. HAVANA. TABLET OVER THE REMAINS.

Although the remains of Columbus were thought to have been removed from Santo Domingo[1] to Havana in 1795, it was not until 1822 that the Cubans erected any funerary memorial or tablet in the cathedral in which they were reinterred. In that year a tablet was erected on the right side of the altar, containing a portrait bust, which Mr. Winsor says is purely ideal in its treatment.[2] Beneath the bust is an inscription which Mr. Ober has paraphrased as follows:

> "O grand Columbus!
> In this urn enshrined
> A thousand centuries thy bones shall guard;
> A thousand ages keep thine image fresh.
> In token of our nation's gratitude."

Illustrations of the tomb may be found in Winsor's *Columbus* and the *History of America*.

1832. NASSAU, NEW PROVIDENCE. THE SMYTH STATUE.

Sir James Carmichael Smyth, who was governor of the Bahamas from 1829 until 1833, presented the town of Nassau on the island of New Providence with a metal statue of Columbus. It was modelled in London in 1831 by an artist named Groggon, and was erected in May, 1832, in front of the government house. The figure, which has since been painted white, is nine feet high, and the pedestal six feet, making a total height of fifteen feet. Upon the side of the pedestal looking toward the sea is the inscription: "Columbus, 1492."

——. CARDENAS, CUBA. THE AVELLANEDA STATUE.

In the centre of the public square at Cardenas, Cuba, stands a heroic statue of Columbus, which was erected by a celebrated Spanish poet and dramatist of the present century, Señora Gertrude Gomez de Avellaneda,

---

[1] There is grave doubt about this supposed removal of the remains of Columbus. It is now believed by many critics that, by some mistake the coffin of Diego, the son of Columbus, or of Luis his grandson, was taken to Havana, and that the coffin of Columbus still remains in the Cathedral at St. Domingo. See paper by Charles Kendall Adams on "Some Recent Discoveries concerning Columbus" in the Annual Report of the American Historical Association for 1891, pp. 89–99. See also Rudolf Cronau's "Amerike: die Geschichte seiner Entdeckung von der ältesten bis auf die neueste Zeit," Lieferung vii.

[2] It was copied from a portrait painted four years before by Bartholemew Basque, but having no resemblance to the descriptions of Columbus given by contemporary writers.

Public Memorials to Columbus. 79

the wife of a former governor of the island. The statue was carved by J. Piguer, of Madrid, and a vignette of it may be found on the title page of a volume entitled *Codice Diplomatico-Americano de Christobal Colon*, published at Havana in 1867. It represents Columbus pointing with his right hand to a globe which he has just unveiled with his left hand.

1880. SANTO DOMINGO. STATUE IN PLAZA.

In the centre of the Plaza in Santo Domingo, in front of the government house and of the cathedral where the remains of Columbus are believed by some to be still resting, stands a heroic figure of Columbus in bronze. It was cast in France, by order of the Dominican government, in 1880. It represents Columbus pointing to the westward, while at the base of the statue is crouched a life-size figure of an Indian girl, who is no other than the unfortunate Anacaona, Caciquess of Veragua, tracing an inscription which reads: "Yllustre y Esclarecido Varon, Don Christoval Colon." An illustration of the statue can be found in Mr. Winsor's *Christopher Columbus*.

1891. WATLING'S ISLAND. "CHICAGO HERALD" MONUMENT.

In July, 1891, representatives of the *Chicago Herald* erected at Watling's Island, in the Bahamas, a small monument to Columbus bearing this inscription: "On this spot Columbus first set foot on the soil of the New World." The memorial is a shaft of coral rock, seven feet high, containing a marble globe. Descriptions and illustrations of the monument may be found in the files of the *Chicago Herald* for the month in which it was set up.

——. HAVANA. STATUE IN THE PALACE.

Upon a lofty pedestal in the court-yard of the palace of the captain-general in Havana, stands a full length heroic figure of Columbus in marble. The sculptor and the date of his work are alike unknown. The face is said to be modelled from accepted portraits of Columbus in the possession of persons in Madrid.

——. HAVANA. BUST IN EL TEMPLETE.

A marble bust of Columbus has been erected upon a column in front of the little chapel, *El Templete*, on the site where the first mass was celebrated on the island of Cuba. The face is said to be unlike all other portraits at present existing.

——. HAVANA. STATUE IN THE PUBLIC LIBRARY.

The Bibliotheca Publica of the Royal Economical Society of the Friends of the Country in Havana, possesses a beautiful piece of statuary by Valtmijana, of Barcelona, Spain. Columbus is portrayed as an old man in chains sitting on the deck of a vessel. An illustration of the work appeared in *The Chautauquan* for September, 1892.

(Projected). COLON, CUBA. STATUE BY MELERO.

"Mr. Miguel Melero, director of the Academy of Painting and Sculpture at Havana, has designed and finished in gypsum a statue of Columbus that will be cast in bronze for the city of Colon, in the state of Matanzas, Cuba. The work is paid for by the generosity of a rich sugar planter of Matanzas."

(Projected). HAVANA. PROPOSED MONUMENT TO THE DISCOVERY.

In June, 1890, the Spanish government, in that spirit of liberality which, has caused the erection of several beautiful memorials in the Old World, determined to do honor to Columbus in the New World also, by the erection of a new tomb and likewise of a monument to the discovery of America. One hundred thousand dollars was appropriated for the two monuments, and after a sharp competition, the designs for the latter were accepted by the Academy of San Fernando from Antonio Susilla, one of Spain's foremost artists. His monument is to be a terrestrial globe, surrounded by a wide band on which appears a suggestion of the worlds *Non plus ultra*. With one stroke of his paw the Lion of Spain has obliterated the first word, thus signifying that, through Columbus, new worlds had been opened up to Europe. The globe rests upon a truncated pyramid, in turn held up by a quadrangular base, flanked by four statues signifying Valor, Study, History, and Naval Art, to which last figure a youth is delivering the mariner's compass. Upon each of the four faces of the base are bas-reliefs representing scenes from the life of Columbus, while upon the pyramid are the arms of Spain, a medallion of Ferdinand and Isabella, and a medallion showing the pennant of the *Santa Maria* floating above a sail. The upper part of the monument is a wave-beaten boat placed upon the Globe, and carrying Columbus, led by Religious Faith. The monument has a total height of 52 feet, the upper group 23 feet, and the four sitting statues, 10 feet each. A description of the designs appeared in the *American Architect* for October 22, 1892, having previously appeared in *El Centenario: Revista Illustrada*.

(Projected). HAVANA. PROPOSED FUNERARY MONUMENT.

The same commission which awarded the design for a monument of the Discovery to Susilla, unanimously adopted the designs of Arturio Mélida for the funerary monument. It consists of a base of Aztec design, as a symbol of the soil upon which Columbus landed, and where his bones now rest.

Upon it, four heralds representing the four kingdoms then composing the Spanish monarchy, sustain the coffer destined to preserve the remains of Columbus. In front Castile and Leon, in an attitude of legitimate pride in their triumph ; in the rear, Aragon and Navarre, who, if they took no part in the glory, have come to share the grief. Upon the plinth the chains laid upon Columbus by the envy of contemporaries, lie hidden beneath the laurels which Spain to-day places upon his tomb, together with the palm of the martyr. Mr. Mélida proposes to make use, in his monument, of the combination of various colored bronzes and alabaster, so often seen in European tombs. The tomb is now being erected in Havana, and a description of it, with illustrations, appeared in the *American Architect* for October 22, 1892, where it was borrowed from *El Centenario: Revista Illustrada*.

(Projected). ISABELLA. SANTO DOMINGO. BOSTON STATUE.

In the summer of 1892, a number of Boston citizens raised, by subscription, a sum sufficient to erect a statue to Columbus on the site of Old Isabella, where the great Admiral planted his first settlement and erected the first church in America. The statue was cast at Chicopee, Mass., from designs furnished to Alois Buyens, the sculptor, by Richard Andrew, a student of the State Normal Art School in Boston. Although completed, the statue has not yet been erected at Isabella, but a replica of it, secured by the city of Boston, was unveiled with appropriate ceremonies on October 21. In making a pedestal for the statue, the committee propose to depart from the usual pedestal of finished granite, and erect one ten feet high from the stones found in the ruins of the old fifteenth century town, thus incorporating in the very walls of the memorial an enduring memento of the early Spanish conquerors. A description of the statue itself can be found in the paragraph on the Boston memorial, and illustrations of it in the *American Architect*, May 28, 1892, and the *Boston Journal*, September 10, 1892.

4. MEXICO AND SOUTH AMERICA.

1850. LIMA, PERU. THE REVELLI STATUE.

A fine Columbian group was erected in 1850 at Lima, Peru, by Salvatore Revelli, an Italian sculptor. The work was done at the expense of the Peruvian government, and represents Columbus in the costume of a courtier of the sixteenth century raising an Indian girl from the ground. The bust is elaborately carved with astronomical and geographical designs. The pedestal is of marble, with an inscription, "A Christoval Colon," upon one face, and upon the other three faces handsome urns for tropical plants. A large lithograph of Revelli's group was executed by the French engraver, Desmaisons.

1870. COLON, PANAMA. EMPRESS EUGÉNIE'S STATUE.

In 1870, the Empress Eugénie, then in the last unfortunate days of her brilliant imperial rule in France, presented a Columbus memorial to the city on the Isthmus of Panama which the Spaniards tried to dedicate to the memory of Columbus, but which American commerce knows under the less poetic and less appropriate name of Aspinwall. The memorial was a replica in bronze of a colossal marble group by Vincente Vela, an Italian sculptor, which was exhibited at the Paris Exposition of 1867. It represents Columbus in the semi-monkish garb, which is often found in the other public memorials of him, with his right hand touching, as if to protect, a half-clad Indian woman crouching at his side. An illustration of the monument was given in *Bulletin No.* 2 of the Bureau of American Republics, and the same cut was afterward used on the title page of later bulletins.

———. COLON, PANAMA. COLUMBUS FOUNTAIN.

In addition to the monument given by the Empress Eugénie, Colon likewise possesses a fountain dedicated to Columbus. On one side of the column of the fountain is a bas-relief in marble of the landing at Guanahani.

1877. MEXICO. THE COLON STATUE.

The monument erected in the city of Mexico, in 1877, to the discovery and settlement of America, and popularly called the "Colon Statue," was the work of Cordier, a French sculptor, residing in Mexico, and the gift to the City of one of her sons, Señor Don Antonio Escandon. It consists of a base of red marble, containing bronze panels, upon which are represented in bas-relief: the arms of Columbus surrounded by a wreath of laurel; the dedication of the monument; and two scenes from the life of the discoverer. Upon this base are placed four life-sized figures in bronze, in a sitting posture. They are Fathers Marchena and Debesa, of Spain, the two priests to whom Columbus was finally indebted for the long-delayed royal favor; and Bartolemeo de las Casas and Father Pedro Gante, the two famous missionaries among the Indians of America. From the midst of these bronze figures rises the red marble pedestal of the statue itself. Columbus is represented in the act of removing with his left hand the veil which hides the Western Hemisphere. Illustrations of the monument may be found in the *American Architect* for April 9, 1887, and October 17, 1888, and in Mr. F. A. Ober's *Travels in Mexico*.

———. MEXICO. NATIONAL MUSEUM STATUE.

In the National Museum at Mexico is a colossal figure of Columbus in marble by Pilar.

Public Memorials to Columbus. 83

——. SANTIAGO, CHILE. MARBLE BUST.

Santiago, the capital of Chile, possesses a marble bust of the discoverer, the face of which is modelled after the countenance made familiar to every one through the engraving of De Bry. A Dutch cap is upon the head of Columbus, and garments of a similar Dutch character complete the bust.

——. VALPARAISO, CHILE. BRONZE STATUE.

In Valparaiso, at an angle of two streets, and in front of one of the handsomest houses in the town, stands a heroic figure of Columbus in bronze. The discoverer is represented in an advancing attitude, holding a cross in his right hand. On the several faces of the pedestal, which is of marble, are suitable inscriptions and representations of nautical instruments.

5. EUROPEAN COUNTRIES.

1821. GENOA. CUSTODIA FOR MANUSCRIPTS.

In 1821 the General Council of the city of Genoa, in order to provide a safe receptacle for several manuscripts of Columbus that had been secured by them in 1816, determined to erect a marble *custodia* in the main hall of the municipal palace. The designs were drawn up by Carlo Barrabbino, official architect of the city at the time, and entrusted for execution to one Peschiera. The *custodia* is a pillar, in which a door of gilded bronze closes the receptacle that contains the relics. Upon the pillar is a bust of Columbus which is purely ideal, Peschiera having discarded all supposed portraits and followed only the written descriptions of the discoverer recorded by his contemporaries. The result was quite unsatisfactory to the people of Genoa. The *custodia* and the bust were engraved for the various editions of Spotorno's publication of the MSS. contained in the pillar, for the Lenox edition of Syllacius, for *Harper's Monthly* for December, 1876, and for Winsor's *Christopher Columbus.*

1862. GENOA. PUBLIC MONUMENT.

The citizens of Genoa dedicated in 1862 the most beautiful of the monuments that have thus far been completed to the memory of their great townsman. The monument stands in the centre of a square near the railway station, and is entirely of marble. The movement for the erection of the memorial began about 1845, but a series of unfortunate accidents delayed its completion until seventeen years later. The contract for it was given to the sculptor Bartolini, who shortly after died; it was then assumed by Freccia who was only able to complete a rough model, which was taken up and finished by Michel Canzio. It consists of a huge, quadrangular pediment, at the angles of which are seated allegorical figures of Religion, Geography, Strength and Wisdom. This supports a large cylindrical pedestal, decorated with ship's prows, upon which is a colossal statue of Columbus, with his left hand upon an anchor. Four bas-reliefs upon the sides of the pediment represent important scenes in the life of the discoverer. There is a model of the monument in the Boston Public Library, a photograph in Harrisse's *Notes on Columbus*, engravings in De Lorgues, Torri, etc., a half-tone in *Harper's Weekly* for June 25, 1892, a cut in *Harper's Monthly* for December, 1876, and a heliotype reproduction in the *American Architect* for August 27, 1887.

1882. PAVIA. BUST IN THE UNIVERSITY.

The University, which Columbus is said to have attended for a short time, in the old Italian town of Pavia, on the Ticino, erected in 1882 in one of its quadrangles, a bust of its former scholar. A full account of the proceedings, with an illustration of the bust itself, was published at Pavia[1] in a little volume of 75 pages.

1884. MADRID. NATIONAL MONUMENT.

In 1884 the King of Spain unveiled in the Spanish capital one of the best monuments to Columbus yet erected. The monument, which stands in one of the principal promenades of the city, consists of a very high column of an elaborate and beautiful design, crowned by a bronze statue of the discoverer, of heroic size. The sculptor, Sunol, has happily succeeded in imparting a peaceful and reverent expression to the countenance of Columbus, who is represented with his left hand outstretched, as if pointing to the lands which he had given to Europe, while his right upholds the furled flag of Spain. The cross-tipped staff of the latter rests upon a miniature globe, and this in turn upon the head of a capstan, about which is coiled a cable. The figure of Columbus is clothed in the costume of the time, and he wears over it a short fur-trimmed coat. A representation of the monument appeared in *The Chautauquan* for November, 1892, and of the statue on the wrapper of Seelye's *Story of Columbus*, published by the Appletons.

1886. COGOLETO, ITALY. HEROIC BUST.

The town of Cogoleto, which has historic claims as the possible birthplace of Columbus, erected in 1886 a heroic bust of him, modelled from the portraits of the Geovian type. The bust stands upon a granite pedestal bearing nautical designs and an appropriate inscription, while upon each

---

[1] Dr. G. Brown Goode, of the Smithsonian Institution, is attempting to collect information on all memorials of Columbus preserved at Pavia.

side is a griffin in marble. An illustration of it appeared in *The Chautauquan* for November, 1892.

1888. BARCELONA. MONUMENT.

On May 2, 1888, the largest monument to Columbus yet erected was unveiled in the city of Barcelona in the presence of Queen Christina and the members of the Cabinet. It is two hundred and forty feet high, and a hydraulic elevator carries visitors to the top. It was the work of several artists, the principal figure being the conception of Rafael Atache, a Catalan sculptor, and its cost, two hundred thousand dollars, was defrayed partly by the city and partly by subscriptions from municipalities, corporations, and individuals. The plan comprises an extensive landing stage at the harbor in front of the city, flanked on either side with a prow of a caravel, one representing the *Pinta* and the other *Nina*, and with a magnificent balustrade adorned with statues of famous explorers. From this rises the lofty and elaborately decorated column, crowned by the colossal figure of Columbus, pointing with his right hand to the newly discovered world, while his left holds a marine chart. The base is of stone, as are also the accessory figures, one group of which represents the provinces of Castile, Aragon, Leon, and Catalonia, the other depicting the patrons and friends of the Admiral. The main shaft and eight colossal lions guarding its base are of iron, while the other figures upon the monument, the panels and their elaborate reliefs, and the representation of Columbus — eighteen feet high and weighing thirty tons—are all bronze, and cast from cannon contributed by the Spanish government. An illustration appeared in *The Chautauquan* for November, 1892, and in Seelye's *Story of Columbus*.

1892. PALOS. MONUMENT TO COLUMBUS AND COMPANIONS.

On the 12th of October, 1892, there was unveiled at Palos, in the presence of Queen Christina and the ministers of state, a magnificent monument erected by the Spanish government in honor of Columbus and the brothers Pinzon and their companions on the first voyage. It represents a fluted Corinthian column, capped by a crown supporting an orb surmounted by a cross. The column rests upon a prismatic support from which protrude four prows of vessels, and the pedestal of the whole is in the form of a tomb, to which broad staircases lead on four sides. On the column are the names of the Pinzon brothers, Martin and Vincente, and under the prows of the vessels is the name Colon, with a complete list of his companions.

1892. GENOA. THE EGG OF COLUMBUS.

The strangest and most unique memorial yet erected to Columbus, if we except a "portable monument" said to have been dedicated by Tammany Hall in 1792, is a representation of the "Egg of Columbus," erected for the Italo-American Exhibition in Genoa during the present year. This extremely bizarre structure is built of brickwork, and measures 36,000 cubic feet, being a little flattened at the base to insure its remaining upright. It is three stories high, and the openings for doors and windows preserve perfectly the contour of the egg. The partition walls are painted in frescoes with scenes relating to the story of Columbus, and the discovery of America. The building is used as a restaurant.

———. GENOA. STATUE AT SUPPOSED BIRTHPLACE.

On the front of the house, No. 9, Via Carlo Alberto, in Genoa, which tradition long believed to be the birthplace of Columbus, a niche in the wall contains a small statue of the great Genoese, with the following inscription: " Dissi, volli, credi, ecco un secondo sorger nuovo dall' onde ignote mondo." This house should be distinguished from No. 37, Vico Dritto Ponticello, also claimed as the birthplace of Columbus, and upon which a tablet was erected in 1887.

———. GENOA. BUST IN THE PALAZZO ROSSO.

The bust of Columbus in the Red Palace was modelled after the so-called Capriola portrait, and was particularly commended by the then Duke of Veragua, a descendant of Columbus. A cut of it appears in *The Chautauquan* for November, 1892.

———. GENOA. STATUE IN THE PALAZZO ROSSO.

In the Red Palace at Genoa there is a statue of Columbus, in which the navigator is represented as standing upon the deck of his ship, pointing out land to his unbelieving sailors, while behind him stands a *padre* with a cross. The pedestal is ornamented with prows of caravels, and on each side of it are allegorical figures representing Discovery and Industry.

———. GENOA. "THE GENIUS OF COLUMBUS."

One of the best of the pieces of sculpture associated with Columbus is the beautiful marble figure called "The Genius of Columbus," in the Royal Palace at Genoa. It represents a winged youth surrounded by a steering wheel, an anchor, cables, and other nautical instruments. An illustration of it appears in *The Chautauquan* for November, 1892.

———. MADRID. STATUE IN THE COLONIAL OFFICES.

The offices of the Minister for the Colonies in Madrid possesses a statue of Columbus executed by J. Samartin, a Spanish sculptor. Its date nor history cannot be ascertained.

——. Madrid. Figure in the Royal Academy.

In the Royal Academy at Madrid is a fine allegorical composition illustrating the Discovery of America, its motto being *Plus Ultra*, or "There is more beyond." It is a female figure upon the back of a lion treading upon globes. The sculptor was J. Gandarias.

——. Rome. Bust in the Capitoline Museum.

In the *Protometeca* of the Capitoline Museum at Rome is an ideal bust of Columbus, the history of which is not known. A replica is in the rooms of the N. Y. Historical Society. The hall called the *Protometeca*, in which the bust is situated, was founded by Pius VII, to contain busts and statues of celebrated Italians, especially those distinguished in the arts and sciences.

(Projected). Barcelona. Triumphal Arch.

In addition to the splendid monument unveiled in 1888, Barcelona is to have an arch commemorative of Columbus. Fifty thousand dollars was appropriated for the purpose in 1890 by the Spanish government, but the liberality of the municipal authorities and of private citizens has largely increased this amount.

(Projected). Granada. Public Monument.

In 1890, the Spanish Government, with the liberality which has recently characterized its erection of memorials to Columbus in the places connected with his career, appropriated $50,000 for the erection of a monument at Granada, to commemorate the discovery of America. The work on the monument was done at a studio in Rome, and the completed model was recently removed from that city to Granada, where it will be unveiled shortly by the Queen Regent of Spain.

(Projected). Rome. Monument to the Vatican.

During the present fourth centennial year of the discovery of America, an international committee has been formed for the erection of a worthy monument to Columbus in the city of Rome. Promises of support have already been received which guarantee the success of the movements. Circulars have been issued asking for universal co-operation among the existing Columbus committees of Europe and America, and for the formation of committees among the Catholics of the world, in order to make the memorial a truly international one. The site chosen for the memorial is such that the statue will face the Vatican. It is possible, however, that this may be changed, and the monument erected within the precincts of St. Peter's.

COLUMBUS PORTRAITS.

The disputed question of the portraits of Columbus has produced a very considerable number of articles in periodicals, and the transactions of learned societies, particularly within the past year. The beginning of the discussion was a paper by Jomard, in 1845, in the *Bulletin de la Société de Géographie*. This was occasioned by a project to raise a monument to Columbus in Genoa, and was followed by Carderera's *Informe sobre los retratos de Cristobal Colon*, printed in 1851, in the *Memorias* of the Royal Academy of History at Madrid. Both papers were reviewed by Isidore Löwenstern, in the *Revue Archélogique*, x, 181. The discussison was closed for the time being, by Feuillet de Conches, in a very able paper in the *Revue contemporaine*, xxiv, 484, but was reopened in Spain by Rios y Rios in a paper published in the first volume of the *Boletín* of the Royal Academy of History, 1877–9. In the same volume will be found two papers, one by Carderera and one by Rosell, bearing upon the same question. The latest Spanish authority is J. M. Asensio in his *Cristobal Colon*, tome 2.

In English, the literature on the subject has mainly been the outcome of the recent study of Columbus. A brief letter by Irving, written in his last years, was printed in the fourth volume of the *Life of Irving*, and in the *Proceedings* of the American Antiquarian Society for April, 1853, an account was given by I. M. Barton, of a portrait recently presented to the Society by himself. A copy of the Yanez portrait, presented to the Wisconsin Historical Society by Governor Fairchild, induced Prof. J. D. Butler to study the history of some of the portraits, and the fruits of his study are given in the *Collections* of that Society, Vol. IX, p. 76 (also printed separately), and in *Lippincott's Magazine* for March, 1883. Cf. also *The Nation*, Nov. 16, 1882. More recently the subject has received careful attention at the hands of Mr. Winsor, Mr. Curtis, and Mrs. M. J. Lamb. In addition to the value of their critical notes, their articles will be found exceedingly interesting because of the abundance of illustrations. Mr. Winsor has presented his views in the *Catalogue of the Ticknor Library*, pp. 94–5, Boston, 1876, in his *History of America*, Vol. II, pp. 69–78, and in his *Christopher Columbus*, pp. 61–70. Mr. Curtis' paper will be found in *The Cosmopolitan*, January and February, 1892; and Mrs. Lamb's, in the *Magazine of American History*, Vol. XXIII, pp. 406–8, XXVI, 241–60. The recent purchase of the Lotto portrait by a citizen of Chicago, has caused the production of several illustrated articles on it, notably one in *The Century* for October, 1892. Judge Daly has recently given an account of Columbus portraits to the New York Historical Society.

RENEWALS: 691-4574

DATE DUE

OCT 21			
MAR 19			
NOV 01			
DEC 12			
MAR 23			
MAY 24			
OCT 22			
JUL 28			
MAY 04			

Demco, Inc. 38-293